IN THE STUDIO
WITH MICHAEL JACKSON

BRUCE SWEDIEN

HAL•LEONARD®

HAL LEONARD BOOKS
NEW YORK

Published in 2009 by Hal Leonard Books
An Imprint of Hal Leonard Corporation
7777 West Bluemound Road
Milwaukee, WI 53213

Trade Book Division Editorial Offices
19 West 21st Street, New York, NY 10010

Photos by Siw Amina Bech, Trond Braaten, David "Mr. Bonzai" Goggin, John Jennings,
Russ Ragsdale, Bea and Bruce Swedien. Every reasonable effort has been made to contact copyright
holders and secure permissions. Omissions can be remedied in future editions.

Printed in the United States of America

Editor: Trond Braaten
Book designer: Kristina Rolander

Library of Congress Cataloging-in-Publication Data is available upon request.

ISBN 978-1-4234-6495-2

www.halleonard.com

IN THE STUDIO
WITH MICHAEL JACKSON

CONTENTS

CHAPTER 2
THE FUTURE OF MUSIC IS IN GOOD HANDS

CHAPTER 3
MORE ON BRUCE SWEDIEN

CHAPTER 4

MORE ABOUT THE RECORDING PROCESS 103

EDITOR'S NOTE

On June 25, 2009, the world was stunned by the sudden death of Michael Jackson. Jackson—child star, international celebrity, and phenomenally gifted performer—had burst through the glass ceiling that looms over successful teen singing stars on the strength of two albums. In 1979 *Off the Wall* established Michael as an independent force, free of the personal and professional limits of the Jackson 5 (later the Jacksons). Three years later, *Thriller* broke all sales records, cemented Jackson's reputation as one of the greatest performers in music history, and earned him the nickname King of Pop.

When the news of Michael's death came, Bruce Swedien was where he is most afternoons—in his recording studio in Ocala, Florida. The man who captured the sound of those records in collaboration with Jackson, producer Quincy Jones, and a host of top L.A. session musicians, was as shocked as the rest of the world. But as he recounts in these pages, to Bruce, Michael Jackson will never represent a troubled human being with a controversial history, but a talent of immense proportions who changed the world of pop music forever.

"Michael was always the consummate artist," Bruce told me shortly after Jackson's death. "He was always totally prepared when he came to the studio. He never had to read the words or the music off the page. He would be up the night before we recorded, learning the lyrics so he could do them from memory."

Bruce helped create the wave of popularity that formed as Jackson branched out from his beginnings as a child and teen star with his family into acting with the film *The Wiz*. The wave crested with the top-selling album of all time, *Thriller*, and began its long descent into the shoreline of changing tastes with *Bad, Invincible, Dangerous,* and *HIStory*. Throughout the process, Bruce saw the physical changes in Michael, even as Bruce dealt with the changes in technology and sonic capabilities that affected the music industry in the '80s and '90s. What didn't change was Michael Jackson's dedication to his art.

"I was surprised at how much Michael knew about many different kinds of music. He knew about the classics and cared deeply for that music. The other musicians—Steve Porcaro, Steve Lukather, all of them—they all admired the living daylights out of Michael, because Michael was an inspiration."

As Bruce told NPR the day after Michael's passing, "Recording was never a static event. We used to record with the lights out in the studio, and I had him on my drum platform. Michael would dance on that as he did the vocals. What an incredible experience. The talent was just indescribably huge."

In the following pages, Bruce examines the big challenges as well as the minutiae of his job—fulfilling the vision of Michael Jackson and Quincy Jones to make records that would combine elements of pop, jazz, and soul into a new kind of music and galvanize the world. It was a vision they would realize beyond their wildest expectations. Looking back through the years that would bring so many new challenges to Michael Jackson, Bruce's view of him remains steadfast.

"The way I want to remember him is as the ultimate musician. He was just fantastic, and he brought a tremendous amount of musical integrity with him every time he came into the studio." The important story—the story of the recordings—follows. And for Bruce there is little else to say.

"The book is complete, and it is the full story of my work with Michael."

On behalf of Hal Leonard Books
Rusty Cutchin
June 2009

FOREWORD: SVENSK

I love to give people that I really like a sobriquet, or nickname. In Bruce Swedien's case, he looks, acts, and eats very much like a "Swedish Man." So I call him "Svensk." (In the Swedish language, Svensk means Swedish man.)

Here's how we first met. Our relationship started one day in 1958 in Chicago. I was on my way to a recording session with Dinah Washington. The session was to take place at Universal Recording Studios at 46 East Walton on the Near North Side, a really well-known state-of -the-art recording studio.

I got out of my taxicab and entered the elevator lobby. Waiting for the elevator was a big, young dude who looked very Scandinavian. He introduced himself: "Hi, I'm Bruce Swedien. We're going to be working together today. I'm the engineer assigned to your session. We're in Studio A. You'll love it!"

That day was the beginning of a loving and lasting relationship. Little did I know at the time that one day I would be in the studio with Bruce, and together with Michael Jackson, Rod Temperton, Jerry Hey, and Greg Phillinganes, who I affectionately call "The A Team," would be recording *Thriller*, the album that literally took the world by storm. Amazing, isn't it?

I know that Bruce and I share the feeling that music is everything. "Music First' is a good statement of how we feel about the subject.

Having just traveled around the entire world three times, I have witnessed, in every country, the results of our collaboration that took place over 25 years ago as I constantly hear these songs being played. They are always played right along with all of the chart-topping records of today and always during the peak hours of radio.

I know it is a Divine statement when the music is captured the same as a director of photography (DP) would capture a shot for film—in a definitive moment. An engineer is the equivalent of the DP, also capturing that definitive moment, and Bruce is truly the "Sonic Superman" of the recording industry and I am blessed that he was on my team. Be sure to check him out.

Quincy Jones
Bel Air, California
December 2000

PREFACE

Back in the early '50s, while I was still trying to string my first sentences together, Bruce Swedien was already carving a niche for himself in the recording studios of America. In fact, I had barely started using a knife and fork when "Big Girls Don't Cry" came wailing over my crystal set at the school canteen in Cleethorpes.

I had no idea who Bruce was and frankly didn't care. After all, they never put the name of the recording engineer on a 45, so who would know? It wasn't until a sunny spring day in early '79 that my education would begin.

Quincy Jones had invited me to Los Angeles to participate in Michael Jackson's first solo album project and when I walked into the control room, my eyes immediately set upon this big bear of a man munching away on Cracker Jacks behind the console. As with most bears, it was hard to determine whether he was content to play along and perhaps share his goodies, or if he was going to jump over the desk and make you the central part of his meal! Fortunately, he just growled a little and fixed me with a quizzical glare, one of many such looks I would learn to understand through the years.

The Bear, of course, was Bruce Swedien, and along with Quincy, the pair of them were about to take me on rollercoaster ride of musical adventure I would never forget.

This book reveals many of the sonic secrets that Bruce developed and utilized in the making of those historic Michael Jackson recordings. However, it is important for the reader to hear between the lines and understand that as well as the technical expertise, these records would never have the same dynamic punch without a huge dollop of Bruce's own special sauce, the amazing qualities that define the man.

There is no doubt he has one of the best pair of ears in the business, but then there's the funk factor. Consider this: here's a guy who ordered two giant "Tail o' the Pup" chili dogs with fries for lunch every day during Michael's sessions.

He would unwrap the meal on the console, take a big greasy mouthful, and carry on working while chili sauce and melted cheese slowly started to drip down the faders. Here's a guy who, thanks to his love of animals, was quite happy to have Michael's ten-foot python Muscles slithering all over the console during the mix of "Thriller," undoubtedly fine tuning Bruce's precious EQs as it went. And here is a guy who never started a mix without first taking out of his well-guarded briefcase half a dozen candy bars and three photographs: one of his beautiful wife

Bea, one of his Great Dane Max, and one of the three of them on a golf cart riding around his beloved horse ranch. He would display them proudly on the desk before beginning. So you see, Bruce always had an ample supply of funk, grease, and love to inject into those amazing mixes.

I am very proud of my association with "The A Team," the great talent of Bruce, Quincy, Michael, and all the fine musicians that worked on those projects. Bruce has brought my songs to life over the years, making them sound as fresh today as the day we recorded them. He is a complete contradiction: on the one hand a technical mastermind, and on the other a kid in a candy store infinitely piddling with each new toy he can lay his hands on. He can be awkward yet patient, eccentric yet conservative, and occasionally a royal pain in the ass! That's why we love him so much. One thing's for sure: with Bruce, there is no bullshit. I couldn't want for a better partner in crime.

Over the years Bruce has taught me tons about sound, but after reading this book I realize I am only just beginning. I can't remember him ever mentioning a "Blumlein Pair" to me! Isn't that something you serve with maple syrup and ice cream?

I've often thought that real genius is the ability to focus completely on every minute detail of a problem, assessing, dissecting, and redefining whilst still being able to step back and consider the big picture before delivering the solution. Such is Bruce Swedien.

At the end of the day, when all of the complex recordings have been committed to tape and the final mix is done, Bruce always pulls out a pair of beaten up old Auratone speakers and listens one more time. You see, he knows that there are millions of kids out there who don't have expensive audio gear; in fact, there is probably one in a high school canteen in Cleethorpes listening on an old crystal set right now! Why shouldn't he get his money's worth? Shouldn't it sound great for him too?

Bruce considers this and makes it happen. That's why he's number one. That's why he makes great records.

Thank you, Bruce. And to all you readers, please read this book with open ears!

Rod Temperton

INTRODUCTION: BRUCE SWEDIEN THROUGH MY EYES

Bruce Swedien was mixing a track for the Brothers Johnson, who were being produced by Quincy Jones. I was in the studio a lot with Q then, singing, arranging, writing, adding my ears to the productions; all in all, I would say I was attending the University of Quincy Jones. This was about 1976, as I recall. (I started with Q in 1973 on *Body Heat*.) We were working with the best board jockeys and the studio scene in L.A. was on fire. Q asked me to stop by and hear a mix that an engineer Q had worked with in Chicago was doing and give him my thoughts. Cool; I had spent many a night with Q at the Westlake mixing room on Wilshire Blvd—looked like a store front. This was in the early stages of computer mixing. Q called the computer Bertha—and Bertha could fuck up a mix like you never knew.

But Q has always been on the forefront. It must have been frustrating to Quincy; I know it was to me—that we had not brought to the grooves what we put on tape. Rhythm section, voices, brass, percussion, strings, and woodwinds would not combine in the mix like we heard when we recorded those elements. So I dropped by in the afternoon expecting to listen to a mix being built like a puzzle. What I heard upon entering, before ever greeting and introducing myself to Bruce, was an experience I had yet to hear. Clarity, punch, warmth, sensuality, balls, balance—as if he reached down into the souls of George and Louis and brought it to our ears. Here was this quiet bear of a man with a Fu Manchu moustache after taxes, who looked like he could have been a lineman for the Chicago Bears, dancing in his seat to the funk and bringing it *all* to us, the listeners.

That was the beginning of 30 years of pure joy and privilege working with Svensk, and only the introduction. His mixes: awesome. But wait! There's more! Then we recorded together. Now, I was a very busy vocal contractor, arranger, and writer and had the pleasure of working with every major act, engineer, and producer in Hollywood and was branching out to New York. Never before or since have I known an artist engineer like Bruce. Personally, he's like a brother, professionally he's like no other.

I was way used to working a mic with singers and working with the best. We all had ideas of how to optimize the quality of our sound for a given song and were always learning new techniques. Then there's Bruce Swedien. We doubled and triple tracked a lot of our vocals. It was "ear candy." Some thought it would make the group sound like more people; however, it is the phasing of the same voices singing the same parts that created the desired sound. We were all accomplished at this — then Bruce added something entirely new and different.

We would perform the first track of our vocals in our usual proximity to the mic (and Bruce *always* had the best mics). Then on the second track we would move back a few feet; the third, a few feet more, and the resulting texture reminded me of the hues of a Rembrandt painting. (Listen to the voices on "Bedtime Story" on the *Sounds & Stuff Like That* album.) Bruce paints when he records and mixes, and like Rembrandt, his artistic qualities are vast, bold, subtle, and recognizable. He has the sensibilities of the most fragile artist, the balls of a bull, the funk sense of the sleaziest bar, and the grandeur of Tchaikovsky.

I have had the privilege of working with Bruce from rhythm section to 100-piece orchestra and in every phase of his recording and mixing, he is as unique as Miró.

Cherokee on Fairfax, 1977. We're recording what became "Ain't We Funkin' Now." At the time, the Bros. Johnson had laid down a killer track (designed by Picasso Jones), but the melody and lyric ideas were still incubating. We took a break and Bruce (after sending us all out of the booth) performed one of his patented 15-minute "rough" mixes (that sound better than anyone else's final mixes). Hearing the qualities and textures of this track, perfectly balanced and each sound optimized in Bruce's rough, I heard in my head the melody and title — "Ain't We Funkin' Now." Thanks, Bruce, for guiding that ship. Then I traveled to New York to put the Brecker Brothers on another track for Q and Bruce gave me explicit instructions of just how he wanted them recorded. I just wanted to please him; he is so meticulous and yet so understanding and accepting of true effort.

And now for my favorite part: observing Bruce as a husband. What a devoted, loving man is this. His wife Bea, one of the sweetest, erudite, loving, and true women I have ever met. Their marriage is one for the ages — a masterpiece. One of the great joys of "living" in the studio with Bruce was hearing about Bea and Max (their Great Dane) and their horses on their ranch. Family, that's what it is. Two hundred plus pounds of *love*, throughout *Sounds & Stuff Like That*, *The Wiz*, artists like Patti Austin, James Ingram, George Benson, and Donna Summer. And a decade with Michael Jackson, each day a joy of making music with the master and hearing it *all*, optimized — loved and caressed by Bruce.

However, if there was something Bruce questioned or didn't like, you could tell. It started with him stroking his moustache and saying, "I don't know about that." And invariably, he would then add a gem, either sonically or through another great thought (he has a lot of those).

I'll never forget playing "She's Out of My Life" for Bea in A&R's lovely studio on 48th Street in New York, while we were working on *The Wiz*. Listen to the mix on Michael's version: how Bruce filled the room and supported Michael with Greg Phillinganes' Rhodes, Larry Carlton's guitar; add Louis Johnson's bass on the bridge along with Johnnie Mandel's strings (not to mention Johnnie's introduction) and the sound of Michael's voice. And I'll certainly *always* glow every time I listen to "Brand New Day," written by our late loved one Luther Vandross (with whom we also worked on *Stuff*). I believe that is my favorite mix of Bruce's, combining the incredible track starting with Steve Gadd on drums. Add Diana Ross; Michael Jackson; Ted Ross; Nipsey Russell; my 70-voice choir, the New York Super Singers (with Patti Austin at the forefront); and a mere 100-piece orchestra, and sit back and listen. Listen to this masterpiece of joy. Thank you, Bruce. Thank you, Quincy. One of my great pleasures is to turn this one up and close my eyes.

However, his recording and mix of the overture on the *Color Purple* album, which I had the pleasure of co-arranging and conducting, may be my favorite too. OK, no favorites—it's just too hard to find a favorite among so many wonderful children. And that's how it felt—making babies, raising them with utmost love, and sending them into the world. Bruce was, at various intervals, loving uncle, father, brother, and playmate to this glorious brood.

Bruce and I are both Quincy Jones graduates and are grateful for the family that Quincy created. So many of us, and yet it feels like we are all such intimate friends. That's what great music and artistry, blended with the love of life and people, will do, and I am so grateful for my years with Bruce. I can see now: I could write a book about these years. Perhaps I will.

I love you, Bruce
Tommy "Nadinola" Bähler

PROLOGUE

The one thing that really strikes me about Bruce, and what I've considered my greatest gain from getting to know him, has been his willingness to give of himself. For him there are no secrets, and because of that he never hides anything that he does—and for being on the receiving end, I'm forever grateful.

Bruce Swedien and I first met in the summer of 1989 at Record One Recording Studios on Ventura Boulevard in Van Nuys, California. Bruce was working with Quincy Jones on Quincy's *Back on the Block* album. I spent one long day in the studio with Bruce and his assistant Brad Sundberg. When the day ended and I was going to say goodbye, Bruce turned to me and asked if I would be interested in coming for a visit to his home? I answered, "Yes indeed," and at the end of the week I got to see Westviking Ranch with all its animals and also get to meet Bea, Bruce's wife, for the first time. Boy, what an impression!

The next turning point came when one of my old friends, a record producer in Norway, Nils B. Kvam, called me and asked me if I could bring a Norwegian power amp, Electrocompaniet, to Bruce to try out. I brought it along, and that connection has stayed with Bruce from *HIStory* through *Invincible* with Michael Jackson, as well as a many other projects.

It is behind the mixing console that Bruce really shines. Just to sit down quietly in the studio when he is working is an amazing experience. He enhances the music at hand in a way that very few are capable of. I've considered myself extremely lucky in being a part of such events.

This book comes directly from the horse's mouth, since Bruce was a central part of what became the seminal albums that Michael Jackson recorded. Music has always been the most important aspect of all the work that Bruce has been involved in.

The proof is in the pudding, so to speak—just listen to the music mentioned in this book, and you'll know as well.

Trond Braaten

IN THE STUDIO
WITH MICHAEL JACKSON

CHAPTER 1

RECORDING MICHAEL JACKSON, ALBUM BY ALBUM

THE ALBUMS

These are the albums this book will cover in great detail: *The Wiz, Off the Wall, E.T. The Extra Terrestrial* (Soundtrack), *Victory*—The Jacksons, *Bad, Dangerous, HIStory, Book I, Invincible*. You will be taken on a tour through all these projects with all the stories involved—all are things that will give you a much better understanding of the creativity at work.

You will find a selection of songs from all these albums that have been put under the microscope—by me. You will find some of the "secrets" that went into the production of all this music. You will find out that there were actually not that many secrets, but a great number of real talents involved. Talent combined with hard work. And I promise you this, dear reader, I won't hold anything back.

Bruce Swedien
Owcala, Florida
March 2008

NOTE: All the Michael Jackson singles are at least top-five hits. Most peaked at number one.

IN THE STUDIO WITH MICHAEL JACKSON

A few years ago I began my *Around the World* lecture tour. The subject matter of the tour is of course, the incredible music that I have had the good fortune to be involved with in the recording studio. I think if I am going to write about that fantastic music, I have to begin by telling the story of how I first met my good friend Quincy Jones. Little did I know that my work with Quincy would lead to me hooking up with Michael Jackson and then later, Rod Temperton. Two more fantastic associations in my musical world of recording.

A winning and unbeatable team— Quincy Jones, Michael Jackson, and me—working magic in the studio.

MEETING QUINCY JONES

I first met Quincy Jones in 1959 at Universal Recording Studios in Chicago. Quincy was about 23, and I had just turned 22. Quincy was a vice president of Mercury Records. He was the youngest executive with a major label in the industry, and the only black executive with a major label in the entire industry.

When we met at Universal Studios in Chicago, we were recording a Dinah Washington album for Mercury. Quincy wrote the arrangements and a guy by the name of Jack Tracy produced the album. So we spent a lot of time together. For the next two to three years, we were doing various Mercury Records projects. We also did something for Norman Granz and a bunch of different labels. We thought alike and our tastes were alike in a lot of things.

In simple terms, we liked to work together. So we did a lot of wonderful projects in Chicago: Dinah Washington, Sarah Vaughn, and many others.

One of the things that's really important to me is the way Quincy and I work in the studio. We have a lot of fun while we're doing a project—and I think it shows in the music. Also, we both loved good food. Everything really good that I've learned about recording music, or about the ethics of music, comes from my experiences with Quincy Jones. Especially about the aesthetics of musical quality. When it comes to superb music, Quincy Jones is Number One with a Bullet!

I am an only child. I never had a sister or a brother. If I could have anyone that I could think of for a brother, that brother would be Quincy Jones. I don't mean "brother," in the rhetorical manner. I mean brother in the familial way. That doesn't mean that Q and I have always agreed with each other. We have had heated arguments resulting from differences of opinion between us. I don't think that brothers always agree either. What has made our relationship last is the fact that true friendship, such as ours, is based on mutual respect. I have the ultimate respect for Quincy, on a musical and a personal level.

And I think he feels the same about me. Quincy Jones is the kind of friend that you could call in the middle of the night, with your most personal problem, either real or imagined, and he would come to your rescue, and your life would be on the right track again. I guess what I am trying to say is that I truly love Quincy. In addition, almost everything that I treasure that I know about recording good music, I have learned from my pal Quincy Jones.

In the studio with Quincy Jones during one of our many sessions with Michael Jackson.

Quincy Jones once said about music and how it works on the emotions, "To get out of whatever was distasteful, unpleasant, uncomfortable, or painful—music could always soothe that. You just crawl in that world and reach in that black hole and grab something beautiful, and it would take you away from all of that."

I'm a very fortunate guy; I went to the University of Quincy Jones! It was Quincy that brought the most wonderful music of my life in the studio, to me to record, first.

MEETING ROD TEMPERTON

Quincy called me one day and asked me to check out the Heatwave album that was such a big success at the time. He said that Heatwave was Rod Temperton's band. I said, "Who?" I was soon to learn who Rod was. Rod Temperton is a British musician and songwriter. He was born in Cleethorpes, on the North Lincolnshire coast of England, in 1949. Rod was one of the original members of the popular funk/disco band, Heatwave. Quincy also said that we were going to be working with Rod on Michael's new album. So I listened to his stuff on the Heatwave record. Wow! I simply loved Rod's musical feeling—everything about it! It was a good band, but the concept of Roddy's arrangements, and tunes, was exceedingly hip. Rod Temperton shone through the music on that album like a bright shining light.

Quincy said to me that he was amazed by the fact that Rod had all of the urban values, including all the ghetto stuff, in place in his music. He very obviously knew American R&B/pop music. He'd been hanging out in the American Army camps playing music, and had been listening to a steady diet of Radio Free Europe. Rod had been absorbing music styles and sounds like a sponge. They all thought that Rod was a black man. When the musicians met Rod Temperton for the first time they all made the comment, "I thought you were *young* and *black*—why, you're *old* and *white*!"

That first day we met (it was a Saturday morning), I was already at Allen Zentz Recording Studio waiting for Rod and Quincy to come from LAX. Rod had flown all night on the red-eye from New York to begin work on Michael Jackson's first solo album. He was working in New York with our old pal Phil Ramone on a new Heatwave album. I think at about the same time he was also working on an album with Karen Carpenter. When Quincy's car pulled into the parking lot at the studio, Quincy and his driver were in the front seat. In the back seat was this exhausted-looking dude in a wrinkled trench coat. His eyes were red-rimmed with fatigue, and he was staring into space. A Marlboro cigarette with a three-inch ash was dangling from his lower lip. That was my first impression of Rod

Temperton. I can see it like it was yesterday. It was in 1978 and we were beginning work in Los Angeles on Michael Jackson's album *Off the Wall.*

Rod is quite different from anyone else I have ever known. For instance, he is an extremely disciplined composer. When he comes to the studio to work, every single small musical detail is on paper or accounted for in Rod's mind. He won't take a day off, or even much of a break, until he feels confident that the music he has brought to life is happy and healthy, and able to breathe on its own.

As far as I am concerned Rod Temperton is a giant in the industry. That's how *Off the Wall* began.

Outside Allen Zentz
Recording Studios:
Quincy Jones,
Rod Temperton,
and myself.

MICHAEL JACKSON

American superstar Michael Jackson was born on the 29th of August, 1958, in Gary, Indiana. He was the seventh of nine children. Michael and his older brothers (Jackie, Tito, Jermaine, and Marlon) were thrust into the spotlight when their father, Joseph Jackson, a steel mill worker, formed a singing group out of his sons and called them The Jackson 5.

Everywhere I go, anywhere in the world, the first questions I am asked are; "What is it like to work with Michael Jackson?" or "What is Michael Jackson really like?" Michael is a bona fide international favorite, and he has been for a long time! He is unquestionably a survivor.

Michael Jackson is the most professional and the most accomplished artist I have ever worked with! And I have worked with the best the music industry has to offer. MJ's musical standards are incredibly high. When I work with Michael, we never settle for a musical production that is "just good enough." Since the *Dangerous* album project, Michael and I have had a saying: "The quality goes in before the name goes on!" In other words, we have to be totally satisfied with the musical and technical quality of our productions before we will put our names on them.

I don't think I have ever worked with another artist that can cause as much excitement as Michael. When Bea and I have traveled with Michael to his concerts, all over the world, we have often thought that we don't know Michael Jackson, the performer, that amazing person on stage. To experience the music that we have recorded together, in a concert, with tens of thousands of people, in a foreign land, and feel the intensity of the emotion of the crowds, is something I can't find the words to describe! For someone like me, who usually only hears the music I'm involved with in the recording studio, to be on tour with Michael is a tremendous event. I get chills just thinking about it!

Michael comes across as a gentle soul. He is very polite. Working with him I always hear him use "please," "thank you," and "you're welcome," in a industry where such pleasantries are not ordinarily used.

HOW I MET MICHAEL JACKSON

The year was 1977. Bea and I were living in Highland Park, Illinois. It was a Sunday night and I was relaxing in the bathtub. Nice hot water, lights down low, tummy full of one of Bea's fantastic Sunday dinners—in other words, very very comfy. I heard the phone ring. Bea answered on the phone. I heard her talking, obviously to a friend. She called out to me, "Honey, it's Quincy." I thought to myself, "I wonder what's cooking with Jones?"

Bea handed me the phone (it was on a long wire—this was before cordless phones). On the other end of the phone was Quincy Jones. Q asked me, "Hey Svensk, want to go to New York and do a musical movie with me?" (Quincy's nickname for me, "Svensk," is actually the Swedish word meaning "Swedish man". The highest honor that Quincy can bestow on a friend is to give him or her a very special Quincy nickname. I value my Q nickname more than words can express.) As a little added inducement he said, "Sidney Lumet will be directing."

Two of the set photographers on *The Wiz* who really stand out in my mind were Berry Berensen and Lou Barrett. Through the course of the production of the film I got to know them both. It was wonderful to work with these very professional folks. Berry Berensen was the sister of actress Marisa Berensen, and she died in one of the hijacked airliners that plunged into the World Trade Center on 9/11. Tragic loss.

Sidney Lumet directed *The Wiz*. This Motown rendition of *The Wizard of Oz* stars Diana Ross playing a soulful Dorothy; Michael Jackson, who plays the Scarecrow; Richard Pryor plays a perfect Wizard of Oz; Nipsey Russell plays a rusty Tinman; Ted Ross plays a delightful Cowardly Lion; and they are accompanied by a cast peppered with R&B stars such as Roberta Flack and Luther Vandross. Rob Cohen produced *The Wiz*. The screenplay was written by Joel Schumacher.

RECORDING MICHAEL'S ALBUMS

In the 1980s, my initial recording medium would have been analog 24 track, two-inch tape, at a tape speed of 30 inches per second. I normally used a record level of approximately 6 db over 185 nano/Webers, or what was commonly referred to in the industry as a record level of "plus three." At that time, I almost always used Dolby SR noise reduction. A bit later, with the high-output recording tape formulations, I rarely used noise reduction when working in the 24-track format. To synchronize two or more tape machines I used SMPTE timecode, 30 frame, non-drop frame, and recorded this on the tape at a level of about minus 15 VU.

At that time, resolvers were not very quick, so I would allow 60 seconds of pre-roll sync-up time at the beginning of each song. This is sometimes referred to as "offset." I always start the SMPTE timecode at zero time base for each song. This gives me a handy time position reference throughout the song. In those days, when I was working in the analog format, I would make several of what I called "work tapes" using the original master SMPTE track and regenerating it through a code restorer so that the timecode was always first-generation quality.

I would then mix the rhythm tracks and make a stereo cue mix on the work tapes using as few tracks as possible. Generally speaking, I would make a stereo mix of the bass, drums, and percussion on a pair of tracks. Then I would make a stereo mix of the keyboards and guitars on a separate pair of tracks. If there was a scratch vocal track, I would transfer a copy of that track across to the work tapes by itself. I used these timecode reference numbers, in little handwritten boxes, that I put on the score that I made for each song. I still use this system today. It is easy, accurate and logical.

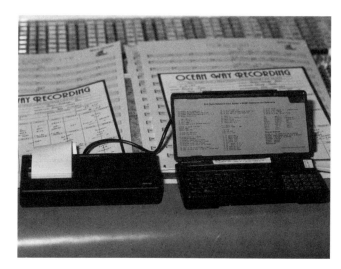

Timecode
calculator
with portable
printer.

Using this technique, in this manner, gave me a virtually unlimited number of tracks to work with. It was not obvious at first, but it soon became apparent to me that with this method, it is possible to do much more than merely obtain additional tracks for overdubbing. Probably the most important advantage of this system is that I can record many more genuine stereophonic images by using pairs of tracks, instead of merely single monophonic tracks. These stereo sound source tracks I kept in discreet pairs until the final mix.

This same true stereophonic thinking has remained with me, virtually unchanged, in the digital age. These true stereo images add much to the depth and clarity of the final production. I have a feeling that this one facet of my production technique contributes more to the overall sonic character of my work than any other single factor. More specifically, the name "Acusonic Recording Process" describes the way that I work with multiple digital and analog multitrack tape machines and SMPTE timecode to generate a virtually unlimited number of recording tracks. Initially I designed the system specifically for the projects that Quincy and I did together. It wasn't very long before I was using this system on every project that I did. Now with a digital audio workstation, the number of tracks can be virtually unlimited, and multiplexing analog multitracks is no longer an issue.

Of course, a young dude by the name of Michael Jackson played the "Scarecrow" in *The Wiz*. While we were working on *The Wiz*, Michael asked Quincy to produce, and me to record and mix, his upcoming solo record. The result, *Off the Wall*, sold a staggering 10 million copies. For Quincy, and me too, new challenges lay just ahead

WORKING WITH MICHAEL JACKSON

Michael Jackson is one of the most professional and the most accomplished artists that I have ever worked with! And I have worked with the best the music industry has to offer. What I can truthfully say is that first and foremost, Michael is an absolute joy to work with. I can't think of another way to express my experience in working with him.

For instance, when we record a vocal, on a song, Michael vocalizes with his vocal coach, Seth Riggs, for at least an hour before he steps up to the microphone to record. I don't mean that Michael vocalizes just once in a while. I mean that he vocalizes every time we record a vocal! To me, that is real dedication. One of the most fascinating things about Michael Jackson is the boundless passion that he has for his music. His enthusiasm for the project at hand is like no one else I have ever worked with.

WORKING WITH MICHAEL AND QUINCY

Working with Quincy and Michael has really been a wonderful experience, because not only do we work together well, but we're really friends. It's a three-man team and our votes count equally. That's the way it works. It's easy. It's wonderful. We had such a good time doing *Off the Wall*, *Thriller*, and *Bad*.

MICHAEL DOES HIS VOCALS ON MY DRUM PLATFORM

Michael and I have always had a definite passion for recording the sound sources in our music in their own acoustical space. We try to make that space as unique as possible. When we were recording "Rock with You" for the *Off the Wall* album, I wanted the drums in this incredible song to have their own unique acoustic space. What should I do? What can I do to create a truly unique space for the drums, in the "Rock with You" soundfield? After thinking about it for some time, the only answer was to have the studio carpenters build me a drum platform, eight feet square, ten inches off the floor. It is very heavily constructed, braced and counter-braced. The surface is natural wood and is unpainted and unvarnished.

Actually, I had been thinking about such an acoustic surface for some time. All I really needed was a good excuse to do it! My pal John Robinson played drums on "Rock with You" on that very same drum platform! I still use it. In fact, not long after we recorded the drums on "Rock with You," I put Michael on my drum platform to record his vocals. I've been using it for his vocals ever since! When Michael does his vocals he dances all through his vocal performances. Actually, I used that same wooden platform to record Jennifer Lopez's vocals and those every artist I have ever worked with!

I use the unpainted plywood surface, of the drum platform to reflect Michael's voice, or whatever sound source I am recording, back to the microphone. In Michael's case, this also preserves the rhythmic effect of him dancing happily away while he sings, as part of his sonic image. I love to have Michael's dancing sounds as part of the vocal sound. Keeping the platform unpainted maintains a surface as porous as possible. The reason that I do this is to keep some reflective surface in the sound-field, but not too much.

Even when we do backgrounds, Michael does little vocal sounds, and snaps his fingers and taps his foot. I keep those sounds as part of the recording. I absolutely love those little sounds as a part of Michael's sonic character. First of all, his time and his rhythm are flawless. I think those little dancing sounds are very important.

MICHAEL IS ALWAYS TOTALLY PREPARED!

I've never run into anybody that works with Michael that doesn't regard it as a pleasant experience. He's really easy to deal with in the studio. For instance, when we record vocals, there are seldom more than four or five takes on the lead vocal. (Although I do remember a couple of songs where we went crazy and did 25 vocal takes.)

Generally speaking, we try not to do more than six vocal takes on a song. Then we'll sit there and select the best of the takes, and make a couple of punches. Michael is always totally prepared. When he comes to the studio to do his vocal, he usually has the melody and the lyrics memorized.

A TYPICAL SESSION WITH MICHAEL JACKSON IS A LOT OF FUN!

A typical session with Michael for me actually can be a lot of fun! On the songs I produced or co-produced with Michael, for instance, it's wonderful. We'll decide on a piece of music to do—and then I kind of get to work on it on my own, a little bit. Once I get a rhythm track down, I'll give Michael a tape of it, and he'll say, "It's great, but let's do *this*." Then I'll go back and work on it some more. So it's kind of an in and out type of thing. Michael is so professional, so wonderful to work with. Doing vocals with Michael is an absolute joy. He's got ears for days, and his pitch is incredible.

Michael is polite and kind. He'll say: "Can I hear a little more piano in the earphones, please?" I turn up the piano in his cue mix, and then he'll say, "Thank you." This is an industry where you don't hear those words a whole lot. So for that reason I totally respect Michael and his musical integrity is so astounding.

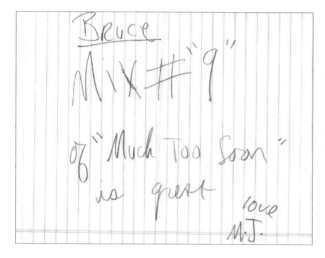

Michael's own handwritten note to me regarding a mix. This has always been one of Michael's ways of communicating comments, ideas, and suggestions during the recording process.

Recording the orchestra for *The Wiz*.

THE WIZ

On *The Wiz*, I was involved not only in the initial music recording for the movie, but in the mixing of the music for picture, on the sound dubbing stage. I also recorded and mixed the soundtrack album. It was a big job with a lot of responsibility. I loved it!

Charlie Smalls composed many of the songs. The music for *The Wiz* was adapted and supervised by Quincy Jones. Quincy Jones, Nick Ashford, and Valerie Simpson wrote and composed music and lyrics for some additional songs.

Some of the all-time favorite recordings of my career came from *The Wiz*. Here are a few:

"Main Title from *The Wiz* (Overture)"
"He's the Wizard (The March of the Munchkins)"
"Glinda's Theme"
"You Can't Win"
"Ease on Down the Road #1"
"Home Medley"

I designed and built a big heavy-duty sound truck, along with my very capable sound crew, Aaron Baron and Larry Dahlstrom. We built it on a two-axle General Motors chassis and frame. It was a 23-foot long truck body. That was the largest chassis and truck frame allowed on the Manhattan streets at the time. We built a complete control room in the van. It had a small 24-input console with a 16-track, two-inch tape machine for playback of the music tracks to the dancers and singers.

We were filming one of the main musical numbers for *The Wiz*, "The "Poppy Girls," on 8th Avenue, when a couple of drunks moved in under my sound truck. It was quite cold, I think it was November, and the two winos lit a fire, under the sound truck, to warm themselves. They pounded on the bottom of the sound truck and yelled up at us, "Be quiet up there, you're makin' too much noise! Why don't you go back to L. A.?" Soon the police removed them. True story. Only in New York.

At that same time Bea was in New York visiting me. She came to hang with me in the sound truck. After the day's work we went to a local hotel ballroom that the producer had booked for feeding the huge film crew dinner. Bea and I sat across from "The Poppy Girls." They were still in makeup, and both Bea and I can vividly recall those three lovely gals, eating a delicious meatloaf dinner, smiling and flashing their long eyelashes at everyone around. Great fun!

We pre-recorded the main musical numbers for *The Wiz* at A&R Studios in New York. Quincy hired the very best musicians in the industry for those sessions. The director, Sidney Lumet, had all sorts of wonderful New York locations in mind to film the musical numbers for the film. I built a special sound playback truck for the project. My goal with the sound playback truck was the in-sync playback of the pre-recorded music for the singers and dancers. Sound travels at a much slower speed than does light, so on each location I had to keep that in mind.

In each scene, if I set up my playback speakers too far from the singers and dancers, the action could appear to be slightly out of sync. Of course, every scene that we did was totally different as well.

I had a lot of fun doing those playbacks all over the New York area. The biggest and toughest assignment was the "Emerald City/Red, Green, and Gold" sequence. The "Emerald City" sequence was shot at the now-destroyed World Trade Center. The space that the set occupied was enormous. It was hundreds of feet across.

When I saw Tony Walton's set design, I asked the assistant director, Burt Harris, to build me a speaker trough as close to the edge of the round dance set perimeter as he could. The film company carpenter did a beautiful job. My crew and I placed the speakers in the trough, facing up, and at no time during the filming is a dancer more than 15 feet from one of my playback speakers. If you look closely at the finished film, you can just barely see my speaker trough and the dancers are all in perfect sync to the music!

When we mixed the music, dialogue, effects, and all the elements to picture, the Dolby Surround Sound in that beautiful dubbing stage added its element of excitement to the end result. It was on *The Wiz* that I began seriously using two or more multitrack tape machines together to realize the production values that Quincy and I were interested in. I did not use SMPTE timecode, because there were very few audio-related SMPTE syncing devices available at that time. I used Mag-Link timecode. It does basically the same thing as SMPTE, but it uses small increments of time (58 seconds) repeated over and over to sync the devices. It worked! What I did was, I recorded a Mag-Link timecode track on both tapes. I then made a physical start mark on the two tapes at the beginning of the track. Then I resolved the tape speed of the two machines with a pair of Mag-Link timecode resolvers, so that they would run at precisely the same speed. By pressing the start buttons on both machines at precisely the same instant, the two machines ran together in perfect sync. It was a real cumbersome, pain-in-the-ass method, but it did give me what, at the time, seemed like a lot of extra tracks to work with.

It was during the recording of the score for *The Wiz* that I came up with the basic analog system of organizing the tracks, the master tapes, and the slave tapes. I call it "multitrack multiplexing." I think the most important feature of this technique, and my method of implementing it, is that I am able to use pairs of tracks, in abundance, to record true stereophonic images, and then retain them in discrete pairs until the final mix. This method also allowed me (when I used analog recording in my work—now, using digital recording, this is no longer an issue) to play the master tape only a few times during the initial stage of the project, and then put it away until the final mix. This feature retains much of the transient response of the analog master tape, by not diminishing those fragile transients due to repeated playing during overdubbing and sweetening.

In those early days of using multiple multitrack tape machines, I would frequently mix recording formats, using my own system of multiplexing multitrack tape machines. analoganaloganalog

Now, of course, I use a high definition digital audio workstation. I think that what the basic digital recording medium does, it does dramatically well. As a recorded music storage medium, digital recording is unparalleled. In the 1970s (when I was working on *The Wiz*), I was recording exclusively on analog tape.

Here's a great little story about when Quincy composed and arranged the score for *The Wiz* on the dining room table in our hotel room. Trust me when I tell you that there is no one else on earth like Quincy Jones! When Quincy and I were in New York working on the movie *The Wiz,* we lived together at the Drake Hotel on Park Avenue for almost a year and a half. We occupied a lovely two-bedroom suite for that period of time. Our rooms consisted of two bedrooms, a living room, and a dining room with a big glass-topped dining room table. We attempted to divide up our domestic duties the best way that we could. Of course, Quincy Jones is an absolutely incredible culinary expert, so he ordered our food when we ate in. My household abilities are far more limited, so I was awarded the laundry and clean clothes duty.

There is one event from that period of time that really stands out in my mind. It was when we were recording the score for the film. The first day for recording the large orchestra sessions of the score was on a Monday. In typical Quincy fashion, he put off composing and orchestrating the music for those sessions until Sunday night. I have seen many world-class film composers do the same thing. I have a feeling that the pressure of the deadline demands, or coerces, maximum creativity. On Sunday evening, Quincy and I had dinner sent up to our rooms. As we ate, I reminded Quincy that we had a huge session at 12:00 noon the next day in A&R Studio A1, with an 80-piece orchestra, to record not only the opening and closing titles, but some of the more dramatic music for the film score.

I also reminded him that he hadn't put a note on manuscript paper yet. He looked at me, smiled and said, "No problem." Of course, this had happened before, so I wasn't extremely concerned. I went to bed. Quincy said to me, "See you in the morning." The music for the orchestra session that was only hours away still existed only in Quincy's imagination. About four in the morning I woke up, and peeked out of my bedroom door. All the lights were on in our apartment! There was Quincy, seated at our dining room table. By this time the dining room table was absolutely covered with music manuscript paper!

Each large sheet of paper had so many notes of music on it that it looked like flies had been pooping on it all night long! Quincy would look at each sheet of music paper and then stare off into space for a bit. To this day, the single most amazing thing that I see in my mind, as I visualize that night, is that there is not a musical instrument anywhere in sight! No piano, nothing! The only music instrument in our apartment that night was between Quincy's ears!

The next morning we left the hotel in a taxi, and headed for the studio at about 9:00 a.m. We walked into big, beautiful Studio A1, at A&R Studios on 57th Street. Quincy handed a huge batch of completed orchestra scores to the small army of music copyists that were set up. The orchestra began arriving at about 11:00 a.m. At about that same time, the parts had all been copied and were handed out to the orchestra. By 12:00 noon, we were ready! The conductor raised his baton, gave the downbeat, and the most glorious dream-like sound that I had ever heard filled the studio! My heart was in my throat! In addition to the fact that this incredible music came from our glass-topped dining room table, what amazed me was that there was not a note out of place anywhere in that entire score! Not one wrong note! Of course Quincy made some minor changes in the orchestration for the recording, but he always does that.

I think that some of Quincy's musical depth comes, in a small part from the fact that in 1957, he settled in Paris, where he studied composition with Nadia Boulanger and Olivier Messiaen, who taught such notables as Maurice Ravel and Aaron Copland. In 1956, Quincy Jones was performing as a trumpeter and music director with the Dizzy Gillespie band on a State Department–sponsored tour of the Middle East and South America. Shortly after his return, he recorded his first albums as a bandleader in his own right for ABC Paramount Records.

UNDER THE MICROSCOPE: "EASE ON DOWN THE ROAD" AND "MAIN TITLE (OVERTURE, PARTS ONE & TWO)"

The music for the musical *The Wiz*, released on October 24, 1978, was recorded using a mix of musicians from the New York Philharmonic and the New York–based jazz group "Stuff," with musicians like Richard Tee on keyboards, Steve Gadd on drums and Eric Gale on guitar.

MUSIC

"Ease on Down the Road"
   Single by Diana Ross and Michael Jackson

"Ease on Down the Road" is a song from the Broadway musical *The Wiz*, best known in its 1978 release as a duet between soul singers and former Motown alums Diana Ross and Michael Jackson. The 1978 duet was released as the theme song of the 1978 film adaptation of *The Wiz*.

Released as a single in the late summer of 1978, the song missed the U.S. Top 40 by one position, peaking at #41 on the Billboard Hot 100. It reached #17 on the Soul Singles chart the same year.

"Main Title (Overture, Part One)"
   (a) "Universal Logo"
   (b) "Wiz: Title"
   (c) "Home"
   (d) "Believe in Yourself"

(e) "He's the Wizard"

(f) "Is This What Feeling Gets?"

"Main Title (Overture, Part Two)"

(a) "Universal Logo"

(b) "Wiz: Title"

RECORDING THE MUSIC SCORE FOR *THE WIZ*

The basic concept of recording the music for *The Wiz* began with the decision to reproduce the music with as wide a frequency range and as great a dynamic range as was possible. To achieve this we decided to use the Dolby Stereophonic Motion Picture Sound System. This high-quality method of reproducing motion-picture sound is very popular in theaters of all sizes. The ultimate technical quality of any motion-picture soundtrack is, of course, only as good as the elements that go into it. It became evident to me early on during the music recording of *The Wiz* that it would be a big advantage to adapt my Acusonic Recording Process to include the motion-picture equipment used in the production of *The Wiz*.

With this in mind, I chose the Mag-Link timecode system to synchronize motion-picture equipment with multiple 24-track master tape recorders. This allowed me the use of traditional film equipment in the production of *The Wiz*; plus, it left Quincy free from the concern of not having enough tracks available to him to realize his rich, kaleidoscopic music scores. The Acusonic Recording Process allows me to preserve stereophonic sound images in the music and carry them through in exact perspective to the final soundtrack and to the soundtrack album.

The author with three 24-track Studer machines.

SOUND CREDITS

Music Recording Engineer: Bruce Swedien
(Pre-recording, production music sound, post-production recording,
    film re-recording, album mixing, special equipment design.)
Assistant Engineer: Ollie Cotton
Technical Coordinator: Aaron J. Baron
Technical Engineering: P. Larry Dahlstrom
Technician: Peter Maiorino
Technician: George Walker
Technician: Mitchell Plotkin
Recording Studio: A & R Recording Studios, New York City
Originally Mastered by: Bernie Grundman, A&M Recordings L.A.

OFF THE WALL

It was 1978 and we went back into the studio, this time in Hollywood, to record
Michael's new solo album, which would be titled *Off the Wall*. I think that at that
time, Michael was very eager to shed his image as a child star. The new album
that Michael and Quincy were planning was definitely Michael's "coming of age"
album.

RECORDING VOCALS WITH MICHAEL

Here's an example of how I have used early reflections to create both presence and depth of field in my recording work with Michael Jackson. I have to say at this point that Michael is not only one of the best vocalists I have ever worked with, but he loves to experiment with sound, and has always been highly supportive and very enthusiastic about my sonic ideas. In addition, Quincy Jones has always allowed me the creative freedom to bring my sonic personality to the music at hand.

When Michael, Quincy, and I have recorded the background vocals and harmonies on all his albums, I'll begin by recording a monophonic melody track with Michael fairly close to the microphone. Of course, Michael sings all the backgrounds himself. Michael is such an expert at doubling his backgrounds and other vocal parts that he even doubles his vibrato rate perfectly! Of course, Michael has absolutely incredible ears. His pitch is flawless!

Next, I'll have him double the same track at the same position at the mic. After that track, I'll have him step back two paces and record a third pass of the same melody with the gain raised to match the level of the previous two. That raises the ratio of early reflections to direct sound. Blended with the first two tracks, this has a wonderful effect.

Finally, I might even have him step back further and record a stereo pass of the same line using the microphones set up in an X-Y pair, or "Blumlein Pair," and blend those tracks in as well. You can hear this technique in action for yourself on Michael's background block harmony vocals on the song "Rock with You" on Michael's *Off the Wall* album, or on the Andrae Crouch choir on the song "Man in the Mirror" on Michael's *Bad* album. This technique tricks the ear into perceiving a depth of field that isn't really there, through the addition of discreet early reflections. If I'm using any reverb on that vocal, I'll make sure that the predelay is long enough so that the reverb doesn't cover those early reflections.

My unquestionably favorite true stereophonic microphone technique is the Blumlein Pair method. This fantastic microphone technique was conceived in the fertile imagination of Alan Dower Blumlein. It is perhaps the best known of all single-point stereo microphone techniques. Almost every engineer has at least heard of a Blumlein Pair, as crossed figure-of-eights (*not* cardioids, as some mistakenly believe) at 90 degrees are commonly known, even though Blumlein himself patented other techniques. It incorporates two bi-directional microphones, one on top of the other to make the capsules as coincident as possible, angled at 90 degrees to each other. It is probably the most candid of all truly stereophonic microphone techniques.

"SHE'S OUT OF MY LIFE"

In 1977, when we were in the Big Apple recording and filming *The Wiz*, our pal Tom Bähler was there with us doing vocal backgrounds and arrangements for the film. We were at A & R studios, on 52nd Street in New York. Bea (my wife) had come to New York to visit me. One day, Quincy and I were in the control room working on something, and I noticed out of the corner of my eye that Tom Bähler was at the piano in the studio, playing and singing a song for Bea. She was obviously very interested in it.

Incidentally, Quincy has one of his very special nicknames for Tom Bähler. Tom Bähler is known to the Quincy Jones gang as "Nad!" "Nad" is short for "Nadinola skin bleaching cream." Tom Bähler is one of the whitest-appearing guys we know. Yet personally and musically, he has the soul of a very elegant black man. That combination makes for an interesting personality. More importantly, it makes for the very best musical character.

The song Nad was playing and singing for Bea was "She's Out of My Life." The lyrics reflect the disintegration of Tom's relationship at the time. Bea still talks about that experience of hearing Tom Bähler's song "She's Out of My Life" for the first time, sung to her by its author, as one of her ultimate musical experiences. The following year, when we were working on Michael's solo album *Off the Wall*, we recorded it with Michael. How Michael could do such a sincere interpretation of the lyric has always puzzled me, because I know it was an experience he had never even thought about.

When we were recording Michael's vocal, he broke down and cried at the end of every take. We recorded about six or seven takes. At the end of each take Michael was sobbing, actually crying. I know he was sincere, because when we finished the last take, Michael was too embarrassed to come in the control room. He just tippy-toed out the back door of the studio, got in his car, and left the studio building. Quincy said to me, "Hey — that sob at the end, that's supposed to be. Leave it on there, leave it there." Of course, I left it there. We didn't see Michael again until a day or two later! I don't know how Michael was relating to the subject of "She's Out of My Life." He'd never had that kind of grown-up relationship with anybody; I don't think so, anyway.

When we were recording the basic rhythm track for "She's Out of My Life" at Cherokee Studios, on Fairfax Boulevard, a block north of the Melrose District, we were recording in Cherokee's Studio Three. At that time Michael absolutely did not curse or say a bad word. He is still pretty much that way. (Although In the past few years I have heard him get mad and say something nasty. I think he's entitled.)

It was the day that we were to record the music track for "She's Out of My Life." It was about 1:00 p. m. We were all in Studio Three at Cherokee Recording Studio. The musicians were slated to arrive at 5:00 p. m. We were rehearsing in the studio. Greg Phillinganes was there playing the Rhodes (perfectly, as usual). Quincy was busy, at the piano making arrangement notes for the song. I was in the studio setting up my mics and all.

Michael was seated at the drums, singing his heart out! Every time we came to the third verse, and the line "Damned indecision and cursed pride," Michael couldn't say the word "damned". He just couldn't bring himself to do it! He would stop singing and, with his foot, hit the bass drum foot pedal as loud as possible! He just couldn't curse! When the rehearsal ended, Quincy quietly told Michael that he would absolutely have to sing the word "damned" for the recording. Michael nodded and said to Q, "I know." He did.

The Michael Jackson album titled *Off the Wall* was released August 10, 1979. It was a big success all over the world, and the first ever album to release a record breaking four Number One singles in the U.S. On the album credits was: "I dedicate this to the year of the child and my mother. — Love M.J."

We recorded most of the rhythm tracks on *Off the Wall* at Allen Zentz recording studios in Hollywood. My assistants were Steve Conger and Rick Ash. We recorded the horns at Westlake Audio in Hollywood. My assistants there were Ed Cherney, Erik Zoebler, Jim Fitzpatrick, and Mitch Gibson. We recorded the strings at Cherokee Studios in Hollywood. My assistant there was Frank "Cheech" D'Amico. I mixed the album *Off the Wall* at Westlake Audio on Wilshire Boulevard in Hollywood, and I mastered it with Bernie Grundman at A&M Recording Studios in L. A. on Tuesday July 17, 1979.

UNDER THE MICROSCOPE: "DON'T STOP 'TIL YOU GET ENOUGH" AND "ROCK WITH YOU"
Off the Wall. Released August 10, 1979.

MUSIC

"Don't Stop 'Til You Get Enough" — 6:04
    By Michael Jackson
    Produced by Quincy Jones and Michael Jackson

Musicians:
    Michael Jackson: Lead and background vocals
    Louis Johnson: Bass

John Robinson: Drums
Greg Phillinganes: Electric piano
David Williams: Guitar
Marlo Henderson: Guitar
Michael Jackson: Percussion
Randy Jackson: Percussion
Richard Heath: Percussion
Paulinho Da Costa: Percussion
Horns arranged by Jerry Hey and performed by the Seawind Horns
Jerry Hey: Trumpet and flugelhorn
Larry Williams: Tenor and alto saxophones and flute
Kim Hutchcroft: Baritone and tenor saxophones and flute
William Reichenbach: Trombone
Gary Grant: Trumpet
Rhythm arrangement by Greg Phillinganes and Michael Jackson
Vocal and percussion arrangements by: Michael Jackson
String arrangement by Ben Wright
Concert master: Gerald Vinci
Additional background vocals by Jim Gilstrap, Augie Johnson, Marionette
    Jenkins, Paulette McWilliams, and Zedric Williams

RECORDING THE "GLASS BOTTLE" PERCUSSION ON "DON'T STOP 'TIL YOU GET ENOUGH"

Here's how it works: I learned long ago that using ribbon mics in the initial recording of percussion tracks definitely makes life easier when it comes to mastering a recording. Listen carefully to Michael and his brothers playing glass bottles on "Don't Stop 'Til You Get Enough" on Michael's *Off the Wall* album. I wanted the glass bottle percussion in this piece of music to have a unique sonic character, and a great deal of impact in the final mix. I used a mic technique that came from my experience learned during the days when it was difficult to put much transient response on a disc.

I used all ribbon (or velocity) microphones to record the glass bottle percussion section. The mics I chose were my RCA 77DXes and my RCA 44BXes. The heavy mass of the ribbon element, suspended in the magnetic field of a ribbon mic, makes it impossible for a ribbon mic to trace the complete transient peak of a percussive sound such as a glass bottle. I'm not so sure that the ear hears that steep, transient wavefront peak either.

If I had used condenser microphones, with the condenser mics' ability to translate the entire transient peak of the bottles, the bottles would have sounded great, played back from tape in the control room, but when it came time to master, such an incredible transient peak would have minimized the overall level (on disc, cassette, or CD) of the entire piece of music. In other words, condenser mics would have compromised the dynamic impact of the sonic image, of the entire piece of music. Check it out.

There is a whole new generation of superb ribbon microphones available to the recordist today. Several of them are absolutely fantastic! We'll talk more about that later. I really started using the new generation of ribbon mics when I recorded Michael's *Invincible* album.

"Rock with You" — 3:40
    By Rod Temperton

Musicians:
    Michael Jackson: Lead and background vocals
    Bobby Watson: Bass
    John Robinson: Drums
    Greg Phillinganes: Synthesizer
    Michael Boddicker: Synthesizer
    David Williams: Guitar
    Marlo Henderson: Guitar
    David "Hawk" Wolinski: Electric piano
    Horns arranged by Jerry Hey and performed by the Seawind Horns
    Jerry Hey: Trumpet and flugelhorn
    Larry Williams: Tenor and alto saxophones and flute
    Kim Hutchcroft: Baritone and tenor saxophones and flute
    William Reichenbach: Trombone
    Gary Grant: Trumpet
    Rhythm and vocal arrangements by Rod Temperton
    Vocal and percussion arrangements by Michael Jackson
    String arrangement by Ben Wright
    Concert Master: Gerald Vinci

My priceless RCA 77DX and RCA 44BX ribbon microphones.
These were the ribbon microphones I used while recording the
glass bottle percussion on "Don't Stop 'Til You Get Enough."

THRILLER

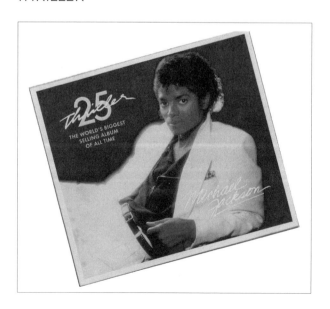

I think I'm very fortunate to have been a part of the making of *Thriller*. It gives me goosebumps to think of some of the sessions. When people ask Quincy if he knew how to surpass the huge success of *Off the Wall*, he always says, "We had to leave space to let God walk through the room!" I think what he is really saying is that there is no spiritual way to connect to the thought of making a bigger album than *Off the Wall*. You just have to focus—and then do it!

"You have to do something that gives you goosebumps." I've asked Quincy about how he felt when we went in the studio to make *Thriller*. He says, "You have to do something that gives you goosebumps and makes you say, 'Yeah man, that really turns me on.' Because if you get turned on, a lot, you've got a good chance of somebody else getting turned on."

In direct contrast, if you say, "Let's put three million dollars down on the table; we gotta make this album three million dollars better than *Off the Wall*," it just doesn't work. They don't talk to each other, creativity and money. Not at all. So you still have to go with God's divining rod, which is the goosebumps, the chills up and down your spine, and everything else. After living through *Off the Wall*, *Thriller*, and *Bad* with Quincy and Michael, I have to agree. I am more proud of the recordings that I have done with Quincy and Michael than any other recordings in my career. I do know that Quincy listened to about 600 songs just to pick 12 for *Thriller*! Now that's dedication! I remember that Rod Temperton submitted about 33 complete demos to Quincy for the project.

I clearly remember one rather interesting event that happened early on the project, while we were working at Westlake's Beautiful Studio D on Beverly Boulevard in Hollywood. A healthy Los Angeles young lady walked slowly by the front window of the studio. That window was made of a one-way glass facing the sidewalk and the street. All of a sudden, while we were watching, she pulled her dress high up over her head. She was wearing absolutely nothing underneath! Quincy, Rod and I got a very good look! We just stood there, gawking! We turned around and there was Michael, devoted Jehovah's witness and all, hiding behind the big Harrison mixing console, getting an eyeful, all the same! True story.

There are nine songs on *Thriller*. Michael wrote four: "The Girl Is Mine" (with Paul McCartney), "Wanna Be Startin' Something," "Beat It," and, of course, the incomparable "Billie Jean." Rod Temperton wrote three: "Baby Be Mine", the title song, "Thriller", and "The Lady in My Life." "Human Nature" was written by Steve Porcaro and John Bettis, and "P.Y.T. (Pretty Young Thing)" was written by James Ingram and Quincy Jones.

When I finished mixing "The Girl Is Mine"—we were at Westlake Audio in Studio D—it was about 8:00 in the evening. I was busy making safety copies of the 1/2-inch mix master in the control room of Studio 'D' at Westlake. I turned around and there was the entire group Fleetwood Mac: Mick Fleetwood, John McVie, Christine McVie, Stevie Nicks, and Lindsey Buckingham. Christine smiled and said to me, "We hear you're making a hit record over here. May we hear it?" At that very moment I noticed that the studio and the control room were almost entirely full of people. It looked like about 100 people had quietly come in while I was busy making safety copies of the master tapes. *And* they were all the most famous music people that you could imagine, beginning with Michael and Paul, Ringo Starr, and so on.

All the heavy-duty music recording artists that were in Hollywood at that moment were there in our studio! I played the master mix for them for the next three hours. They were having a great time, dancing, acting ignorant and all. Michael hid with me in the control room, but he had a huge smile on his face, because everyone was having a great time!

For me, the centerpiece of the album *Thriller* is, of course the title song. The song "Thriller" actually began life as "Starlight." Somewhere in my tape collection I have that demo of "Starlight" with Rod singing the lead vocal! I love "Thriller" the most because there's more of my imagination in the soundfield of it than any other song I have ever recorded. "Thriller" is a definite study in contrasts and layers. Yet there is a great deal of clarity in this recording. I used an entire 24-track reel just to build the spooky intro. I read somewhere recently that Rod has become one of the most successful British songwriters of all time. Great albums always start with great songs.

In the studio listening to a mix through my JBL 4310s.

From the control room at Westlake Studio D during *Thriller*.

One handwritten note from Michael during the project.

Bruce thanks for putting up with all my craziness I love you & "B"

the NOVA BEAM will Be here in several DAys for you also

THANX Mich

P.S. please Bruce MAKe sure our CAssette level Blows every Album AwAy. THANX

The Grammy Award to *Thriller* for album of the year.

DAVID HARRISON

The first session on *Thriller* was at 12:00 noon on Wednesday April 14, 1982. It was at Westlake Audio's beautiful new Studio A on Beverly Boulevard in Hollywood. That first session was Michael Jackson and Paul McCartney recording "The Girl Is Mine."

It was on this session, with Michael and Paul McCartney, that I first used a Harrison 32 Series music recording console. Westlake Audio Recording Studios had just installed a new Harrison 3232 series 40 input music mixing desk in Studio A. Little did I know that this would be a very happy relationship that has lasted until the present time. In fact, I still own and happily use a Harrison 3232 series music recording console in my own beautiful little music studio at home.

Of course, I have recorded and mixed on every available type of music desk that there is in this industry. However, once I had used the marvelous-sounding Harrison 32 series desk, I was convinced that this was the sound in a mixing desk for me! There is something very warm and rich about the sound of the 32 series Harrison that I haven't heard in any other large-format mixing desk.

I was so impressed with the Harrison 3232 that I wanted to get to know its designer, David Harrison, better. I called him in Nashville, and we struck up a friendship that lasted many years. His company delivered the first Harrison console in 1975, marking a milestone in a long history of technological breakthroughs by Harrison engineers.

One day Dave Harrison called me and asked if I could help him with the final design of the line output stage of the then-new Harrison 32c series music mixing desk. I said, "Yes, of course, it would be an honor." I was working on Michael's *Thriller* album at the time. A couple of days later, Dave and an assistant arrived early in the morning at Westlake Audio and proceeded to install three different output amplifiers for the 32c music mixing desk that had very recently been installed in Studio A.

A master switch that Dave installed on the top plate of the desk selected the three output amplifiers. I could only listen to one at a time while I was recording and mixing. Of course Dave had matched the gain of the three output amps perfectly so that a discrepancy in volume level between units could not be interpreted by me as a change in sound quality. He had made up a small hand-written paper form for me to keep a rough record of which switch position I was listening to and how I perceived the sound of it. One day he arrived, early in the morning, and removed all the stuff, collected my little paper form, and I never heard any more about it. Also in 1981 and 1982, during the time that I worked on Michael's album *Thriller,* Dave Harrison called me every Friday evening and asked me, "Bruce, is there anything that you need?" Now that's dedication!

David Harrison died in 1992. I miss him a great deal every time I reminisce about Michael's *Thriller* album. I heard something in his wonderful 3232c series music mixing desk that I hadn't heard before, and haven't heard since. Perhaps it is due in part to the simplicity of its signal path. The EQ of this warm-sounding desk is legendary. I simply love it!

My own Harrison 3232 at my little home studio.

THE OTHER DAY I READ THE FOLLOWING
IN AN INDUSTRY MAGAZINE

"The two invisible men from Michael Jackson's heyday were engineer Bruce Swedien, who would often record as many as 100 (yes, 100) tracks, using various musicians, and assemble a thick, Phil Spector-ish wall of sound that gave Jackson's work a uniquely meaty feel (and still does — Swedien is Jackson's engineer).

The other invisible man was a guy named Rod Temperton. Temperton — a man most people have never seen, so he could be, like, at the supermarket buying Cheerios and you'd never know — is the killer writer of such megahits as Heatwave's 'Always and Forever.'"

I've never thought of Roddy and myself as invisible. Perhaps so, though.

MIXING *THRILLER*

When we first thought we had finished mixing *Thriller*, the album, we had much too much playing time on the sides of the LP. Of course, *Thriller* came out in the days of the long-playing album. I know it was over 25 minutes per side. Of course on LPs, if you have too much time on a side, it minimizes the volume level, and low frequency response, that you can put on the record during mastering. In those days, 18 minutes per side on an LP was just right for good sound. We were way over! I kept telling the guys (Michael, Quincy, and Rod) that the sides are too long for good sound! They didn't listen to me! Quincy even says that one time I got really mad, and slammed the control room door! I don't remember that! Q says that it's true. Of course, I am very passionate about my work.

I took the tapes to Bernie Grundman Mastering to master them, and returned to Westlake Studios to play the mastered album. Quincy had scheduled a meeting with Michael, himself, Rod Temperton, Freddy De Mann (Michael's manager, at the time), myself, and all the big moguls from Epic Records. The Epic folks had two big bottles of champagne on ice to toast *Thriller*. Needless to say, Epic Records was very anxious to get their hands on *Thriller*!

I played the reference LPs in the control room. We listened, and the sound on the LP was dog doo. It was horrible. Quincy remembers that we had 28 minutes on each side. I felt like shouting *"I told you so!"* The Epic dudes were popping corks, but out of the corner of my eye, I saw Michael sneak out of the control room, and go to the other studio, across the hall. Quincy saw him too and followed him. I was next. Then Rod and Freddy. I remember that Michael was crying; he was heartbroken. Again, I felt like shouting *"I told you so!"* And so, Quincy, Freddy De Mann, Rod, myself, all of us, and Michael just sat there.

Quincy Jones, as always, came to the rescue! Quincy said, "Let's take two days off, come back in, and finish one song a day." We had nine songs on the album.

"The Girl Is Mine" was already out, so we needed eight more days. To quote Quincy Jones: "And we put those babies, put 'em in the pocket, man. That was it. It was over, over!" We edited down the songs, we remixed and overdubbed. In eight days I was back at Bernie Grundman Mastering. Now the sound on the LP was screamin'!

The rest is history. The *Guinness Book of World Records* listed *Thriller* as the biggest-selling album of all time, and by October 1984, it had sold over 20 million copies in the U.S. alone. It remains the biggest-selling album to this day. At the World Music Awards in November 2006, a Guinness World Records representative presented Jackson with a certificate for *Thriller* for achieving worldwide sales of 104 million. Nothing will ever top this album!

I think that *Thriller* was such a phenomenal success because the music that was on it reached everyone! Great songs! Killer songs! *Thriller* went everywhere; it appeals to people from eight to 80. Just think: a young black kid, being the idol of so many millions of kids all over the world. That never happened before.

Here is a photo of Quincy and I the day we started the mix of *Thriller*. On my right is Ed Cherney. The Studio is Westlake Audio Studio A on Beverly Boulevard in L.A. Look at the grin on Q's face—he was definitely diggin' it!

ELVIS IS THE GUY

Something else happened with *Thriller* that I find very interesting. Up until the tremendous success of *Thriller*, I would hear my white friends say, "Ray Charles is OK, but Elvis is the guy, you know!" or, "Stevie Wonder is cool, but check out Billy Joel!" Well, they can't say that anymore. I am intensely proud of being a part of the making of Michael Jackson's *Thriller*, the biggest selling album in the history of recorded music!!

The Michael Jackson album titled *Thriller* was released by Epic Records:

Produced by Quincy Jones
Co-produced by Michael Jackson
Recorded and mixed by Bruce Swedien, using the Acusonic Recording Process
Technical engineer: Matt Forger

Assistant engineer: Steve Bates
Additional sound sources recorded by Humberto Gatica and Matt Forger
Additional sound sources recorded at Ocean Way Recording Studios,
    Los Angeles, CA
Assistant sngineer: Mark Eitel
Recorded at Westlake Audio, Los Angeles, CA
Eddie Van Halen's guitar solo on "Beat It" recorded by Donn Landee
On the album credits: "This album is lovingly dedicated to Katherine Jackson"
Rap on the title song "Thriller" performed by Vincent Price

I mixed *Thriller* at Westlake Audio on Beverly Boulevard in Hollywood. I
mastered *Thriller* with Bernie Grundman on Thursday November 11, 1982.

Bernie Grundman of
Bernie Grundman
Mastering in Hollywood,
California.

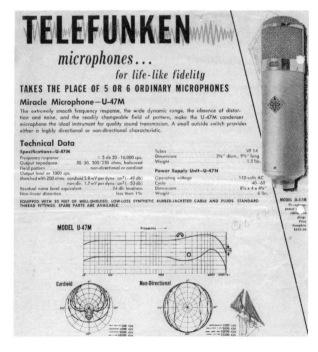

Just imagine, if you can, that this microphone has been used by me on vocals by Joe Williams with the Count Basie Orchestra, Sarah Vaughn, Patti Austin, James Ingram, and Jennifer Lopez, as well as on all of Michael's albums. It's been around since the early fifties and it only shows just how mature microphone technique was at that time already—this is a hard one to beat for vocals! Reprinted here is the original spec sheet from the time when I bought my Telefunken U-47 during the first part of the fifties.

Here's a photo of Max and me, all duded up, going to the studio to work on the intro to "Thriller."

UNDER THE MICROSCOPE: "THRILLER" AND "BILLIE JEAN"

Thriller. Released November 30, 1982. It is the biggest selling album in the history of recorded music.

MUSIC

"Thriller" — 5:57
> By Rod Temperton
> Lyrics sung by Michael Jackson
> Featuring rap performed by Vincent Price

THRILLER INTRO

I had a large dog whose name was Max. He was a Great Dane. Very large—close to two hundred pounds! I tried for several days to get Max to do the wolf howls that we wanted for the intro on "Thriller." I really wanted to have Max's voice in the intro of "Thriller." However, Max didn't want to be the "wolf" on the intro to "Thriller!" We bribed Max with hamburgers, we put him out by the barn to listen to the coyotes at night, but Max wasn't interested in being part of "Thriller." In the end, we had to have Michael do the wolf howls.

In the second intro section (after the scary introduction), I tried to create a low-end-of-the-spectrum illusion, by starting the kick drum (that appears only in that part of the intro) with very minimal low frequency response on it. The ear quickly adjusts to that spectral response. Then, when the bass and the real kick drum come in, with ass-kicking low end, the impact is startling!! Listen to "Thriller" sometime with these thoughts in mind.

As usual, Quincy hired the greatest musicians on the planet to play on "Thriller."

"Thriller" intro track sheet.

The rhythm section:
    Greg Phillinganes, Rod Temperton, and Brian Banks: Synthesizers and rhythm
    Synthesizer programming: Anthony Marinelli
    Guitar: David Williams
    Effects by Bruce Cannon and Bruce Swedien
    The Seawind Horns:
    Jerry Hey: Trumpet and flugelhorn
    Gary Grant: Trumpet and flugelhorn
    Larry Williams: Saxophone and flute
    Bill Reichenbach: Trombone

Musicians:
    Michael Jackson: Solo and background vocals
    Greg Phillinganes , Rod Temperton, and Brian Banks: Synthesizers
    Anthony Marinelli: Synthesizer programming
    David Williams: Guitar
    Jerry Hey: Trumpet and Flugelhorn
    Gary Grant: Trumpet and Flugelhorn
    Larry Williams: Sax and Flute
    Bill Reichenbach: Trombone
    Vocal, rhythm, and synthesizer arrangement by Rod Temperton
    Horn arrangement by Jerry Hey
    Effects by Bruce Cannon and Bruce Swedien

The Vincent Price rap on "Thriller"

When I begin reminiscing about recording the song "Thriller," one of the first things that comes to mind is the Vincent Price rap. Quincy's wife, Peggy Lipton, knew Vincent Price. So Quincy and Peggy got it together and called him. Vincent said he would love to do it. I remember Rod's idea, at first, was that Vincent would just talk some horror talk—the type of lines he would deliver in some of his famous roles. Well, the night before the session with Vincent Price, I remember Quincy and Rod on the phone, talking excitedly about something to do with Vincent's part in "Thriller." I was getting the track ready for Vincent to overdub on, so I only overheard bits and pieces of Quincy and Rod's conversation.

The next day at about 12:00 noon, Quincy showed up at the studio, looking like the cat that swallowed the canary! Q looked at me and said, "Svensk, Vincent Price is going to be here at 2:00 p.m.! Rod is writing Vincent's rap in the taxicab on the way here to the studio!" Quincy told me, "I don't think that Vincent has ever been on a pop record before. This should be interesting." I get chills just thinking about it!

The next thing I knew, Rod came roaring into the control room with several sheets of paper in one hand, and a Marlboro cigarette with a two-inch ash ready to fall over the floor, in his mouth. Out of breath, Roddy said to me, "Bruce, quick—he's here! I saw a car pull up, and it was Vincent Price! He's on his way in!" He thrust the papers into my hand and said, "Give these to the secretary—have her photocopy these quick!" This was done, we put the "Thriller Rap" lyrics on the music stand. Vincent walked in, sat down on his chair, off he went, and it was all done in about two hours.

I used the same microphone setup as I used on Michael: my favorite Shure SM-7. Vincent Price had never used earphones in his work before. He reluctantly put them on, and when the music track for "Thriller" started, he jumped up from his stool with a very startled look on his face. I know he had never heard anything like that before. He asked Rod Temperton to come out in the studio with him and help him by cueing him where to come in and speak his verses. Rod actually wrote three verses for Vincent to do for "Thriller." We recorded all three but only used two. I have that unused verse in my tapes somewhere.

Vincent experienced a huge resurgence in his career, commensurate with the incredible success of "Thriller." About six months after the release of "Thriller," Vincent appeared on the Johnny Carson *Tonight Show*. He talked about being in Paris, walking down the street and having a group of young people recognize him and chase him down the street to get his autograph.

To me, the miraculous thing about the Vincent Price rap on "Thriller" is that Rod Temperton wrote a brilliant Edgar Allan Poe–style spiel in the taxicab on the way to the session! When the chips are down, that's when you find out what true genius is all about! Of course, speaking of unquestionable genius, Vincent's performance was remarkable! Obviously, Vincent Price was in his element on "Thriller"—timing, inflection—and he did it in two takes! Michael's vocals are more than wonderful as well. What an experience!

"Billie Jean"—4:57
    by Michael Jackson

The year is 1982. The song is "Billie Jean." "Billie Jean" is a perfect example of what happened when I sat around dreaming awhile, about combining different recording techniques to produce a unique musical canvas, with a tremendous "sonic personality."

I recorded the drums (played by my pal N'Dugu) with as tight and powerful a drum sound as I could. Of course I put N'Dugu's drum set on my plywood drum platform. Also at this time, I had a special kick drum cover made that covers the entire front of the kick drum. There's a slot in the cover with a zipper, where the mic fits through. When the kick drum mic is in place, in the slot in my drum cover, I zip the opening tight around the mic. I brought in my good friend George Massenburg's spectacular sounding, portable, 12-channel mixing console, and used it to record the rhythm section. With it I recorded the bass, drums, and guitars on my analog 16-track, with no noise reduction equipment in the way of that fantastic sound!

"Billie Jean" may be the most personal song that Michael has ever written: a guilt-inspired paternity drama influenced by Michael's run-ins with delusional female fans. "Billie Jean" is such a superb song! Michael told us: "It's about a girl that climbed over the wall at my house, and was lounging out there, by the swimming pool. She was laying out there, near the pool, lounging—hangin' out—with shades on, in her bathing suit." One morning she just showed up! Kind of like a stalker, almost. She had accused Michael of being the father of *one* of her twins. Is that possible? I don't think so.

"Billie Jean" was released in January 1983. The song topped the Billboard Hot 100 for seven weeks. It held the No. 1 spot on the R&B chart for nine weeks and sold more than a million singles. "Billie Jean" destroyed MTV's color line. "Billie Jean" also saw a former kid singing star coming of age. This was the moment when he blossomed into the late 20th century's dominant pop icon, Michael Jackson. "Billie Jean" is a song that, to this day, remains one of the most sonically arresting songs ever on Top 40 radio. In 1983 no one had ever heard anything quite like it.

"When we recorded "Billie Jean," Quincy told me, "Svensk, this piece of music has to have the most unique sonic personality of anything that we have ever recorded." I had Michael sing some of his vocal overdubs through a five-foot-long cardboard tube. Quincy brought in jazz saxophonist Tom Scott to play a very unusual instrument, the Lyricon, a wind-controlled analog synthesizer whose unique, trumpet-like lines are subtly woven through the track. Bassist Louis Johnson played a Yamaha bass with an ideal sound for "Billie Jean."

I think it was Michael's dancing, as much as his singing, that propelled the "Billie Jean" phenomenon. On May 16, 1983, more than 50 million viewers watched Michael debut his famous moonwalk in a mesmerizing performance on the *Motown 25* television special. I don't know about you, but I have never seen anything like that on television before or since. Then there was the "Billie Jean" video, in which Michael dances through a fantasy cityscape, with a sidewalk that lights up like a disco floor underfoot.

MTV almost never aired videos by black performers, and when they refused to show "Billie Jean," CBS Records president Walter Yetnikoff went ballistic. He said to MTV, "I'm pulling everything we have off the air, all our product. I'm not going to give you any more videos. And I'm going to go public and fucking tell them about the fact you don't want to play music by a black guy!" "Billie Jean" was immediately put in heavy rotation on MTV. In my estimation, "Billie Jean" is a perfect example of what I call "sonic personality." I don't think there are many recordings where all you need to hear is the first few drum beats, and you instantly know what song it is.

Musicians:
Michael Jackson: Solo and background vocals
Greg Phillinganes: Rhodes, synthesizer
Greg Smith: Synthesizer
Bill Wolfer: Synthesizer, synthesizer programming
David Williams: Guitar
Louis Johnson: Bass
N'Dugu Chancler: Drums
Michael Boddicker: Emulator
Vocal, rhythm, and synthesizer arrangement by Michael Jackson
String arrangement by Jerry Hey
Strings conducted by Jeremy Lubbock

JOHN Q. PUBLIC'S LISTENING ABILITY HAS IMPROVED!

It seems that the listening ability, or aural acuity, of the record-buying public has advanced a great deal in the last decades. In the late 1970s and the early part of the 1980s, the attention of record buyers was momentarily sidetracked. Video games became a huge, almost overnight, success. In the late 1970s, I heard some people say that recorded popular music couldn't possibly survive the attention that the young people were paying to video arcades and home video games.

Record sales had been declining by considerable numbers since the middle 1970s. There are several facets to the explanation of that situation. There is not one single reason. There are basically two factors, in my opinion, that were important at that time. The first element is that popular music in the late 1970s, with a few exceptions, had been going downhill in musical quality. Recording artists had become financially fat, artistically lazy, and ethically complacent. Many of the recording groups and acts that had had a measure of success at that time were going into the studio with little or no thought or preparation. It seems that somewhere along the way, our standards had slipped. Many recording artists would put most anything out just to satisfy a recording company contract, or to have a record before the public, quality and music be damned! It's no wonder that the record stores were frequently empty. As Samuel Goldwyn once said about the movie business, "People were staying away in droves!"

Quincy said: "We've got to get people back in the record stores!" Something had to be done to get people to want to go back in the record stores to buy records. I remember Quincy Jones solemnly saying, as we entered the studio to begin work on Michael Jackson's *Thriller* album, "We're here to make people want to go to the record stores again!" He was right, of course. I have never, in my life, seen a group of people so dedicated to one project. Starting with Michael, Quincy, Rod, and myself, everyone involved at every level on *Thriller* gave at least 110% all day, every single day. It worked!

With the phenomenon of Michael Jackson's incredible performances and compositions, and Quincy's impeccable musical taste and direction, all I had to do was use my imagination and paint the widest sonic canvasses of my life. *Thriller* encouraged people to get out of the video arcades and into the record stores and buy records again, in large numbers, as well. Not only did the record-buying public go into the record stores to buy *Thriller*, but while they were there, they bought other good records as well.

I think probably the truth in the explanation is the fact that music is organic in the human psyche. Music, and the images that it conjures in the imagination, is the oldest, wildest and richest video game in humanity. Quality music, we found, could be much more important to us than trendy video images and sounds. I think the musical and technical quality, coupled with the incredible musical depth of *Thriller,* made it a seminal event in the history of recorded music. We, in the industry, have a tendency to think of success in popular recorded music, only in terms of units sold and sales grosses. Indeed, the units sold and the legendary sales figures of *Thriller* were ultimately the greatest possible mandate of a music-loving public.

I am sure, in years to come, historians will say that *Thriller* was definitely as big or bigger a success musically and artistically as it was financially. I absolutely love *Off the Wall,* but *Thriller* took us to another level: a whole new place in recorded popular music! For that reason, *Thriller* will always have a very special place in my heart.

VICTORY

The year is 1984. The month is June. *Thriller,* by this time, was off and running. The *Thriller* album was shattering all kinds of records, and well on its way to becoming the biggest-selling album of all time. Michael called me one day and said that we were going to be recording two new songs on the new Jacksons album. He told me that we would be recording a new song of his with Mick Jagger in New York. That fantastic song was, of course "State of Shock," a duet between Michael and Mick. It has a fantastically strong, rock and roll edge and is quite different from the more pop-oriented songs that Michael did with Paul

McCartney. The other song was "Be Not Always," a beautiful ballad with a bit of a message for Michael's fans. I love this song.

At the same time, the hottest news in the music business was that Michael and his brothers were going to be doing an album together for the first time since 1975. Jermaine was returning to the group so that all six brothers would appear on an album together for the very first time. Jermaine had not recorded or toured with the Jacksons since the group left Motown in 1975.

A major tour, titled *The Victory Tour*, was in the planning stages. *The Victory Tour* ended up being a music tour of the United States and Canada by the Jacksons. It started July 6, 1984 and ended December 9, 1984. *The Victory Tour* included 55 concerts played to about two million fans. It was the biggest tour any group had ever made at the time. "State of Shock" was the biggest hit from the Jacksons' *Victory* album, reaching number three on the Billboard Hot 100 chart and number four on the Billboard R&B Singles chart. The *Victory* album became the biggest seller and highest-charting album of the Jacksons' career, leveling out at number four. It was also the first and only album in the Jacksons' career to include all six Jackson brothers together on one record.

The day that "State of Shock" was released in Los Angeles, an L. A. disk jockey played the song non-stop for 24 hours. His explanation was, "I figured those guys needed the money." While we were working on "State of Shock" at A & R Studios in New York, Mick and I got a jones for White Castle hamburgers. So Bea and one of the security guards drove over to Queens and got 50 White Castle hamburgers for us. Aaah, heaven! (Michael calls White Castle hamburgers "mouse burgers!")

UNDER THE MICROSCOPE: "STATE OF SHOCK"
Victory—The Jacksons Album. Released October 30, 1984.

MUSIC

"State of Shock" (Michael's excellent duet with Mick Jagger)
    Produced by Michael Jackson
    Music written, composed, and arranged by Michael Jackson
    Lyrics by Michael Jackson and Randy Hansen
    Produced by Michael Jackson
    Lead vocals by Michael Jackson and Mick Jagger
    Background vocals by Jackie, Marlon, and Michael Jackson

Musicians:
    Michael Jackson: *Claps and Linn programming*
    David Williams: *Guitar and bass*
    Paulinho DaCosta: *Percussion*

Recorded and mixed by Bruce Swedien,
  from the original 16-track engineered by Brent Averill
  Assisted by Matt Forger and Ollie Cotton (NY)
  Recorded at Westlake Audio and A & R Recording Studios (NY)
  Mixed by Bruce Swedien at Westlake Audio
  Technical director: Matt Forger
  Project coordinators: Nelson Hayes and Shari Dub
  Vocal consultant: Seth Riggs

Seth Riggs, Michael's vocal mentor: the man behind the "speech-level singing method." Michael always did prepare himself thoroughly before he put down any vocals at all in the studio by doing exercises for several hours at times before any singing was done. Seth Riggs was important in teaching Michael how to most effectively work his voice.

BAD

The year is 1987. Quincy, Michael and I are comfortably ensconced in Westlake Audio's beautiful new Studio D, on Santa Monica Boulevard in Los Angeles, recording Michael's new solo album *Bad*. The first session on the *Bad* album was done on Monday January 5, 1987.

Westlake Audio had very recently installed a brand-new, quite large Harrison MR-2 desk of 56 inputs in their lovely new Studio D. For the time, 56 inputs was an extremely large mixing desk. I wondered to myself, "I sure hope this new Harrison sounds as good as the 32c series." Well, I soon found out that it sounded absolutely fantastic! I should have known.

There are eleven songs on *Bad*:

"Bad"
"The Way You Make Me Feel"
"Speed Demon"
"Liberian Girl"
"Just Good Friends"
"Another Part of Me"
"Man in the Mirror"
"I Just Can't Stop Loving You"
"Dirty Diana"
"Smooth Criminal"
"Leave Me Alone"

When we started work on the album, the title song had a working title of "Pee!" Now that I think about it, I think we even called the album *Pee* as well. The name "Pee" was a Quincy name, of course. Quincy told me that the title song, (at that time named "Pee") was going to be a duet for Michael and Prince. I remember that Quincy said that the concept for the duet video was a fight scene, a street fight thing, with Prince coming to kick Michael's ass. Can you imagine the video with Michael's opening lyric being sung by him to Prince: "Your butt is mine?" I was there for a couple of the meetings with Prince and Michael, Quincy and all. Personally, I think that after meeting with Michael and Quincy, Prince realized that he couldn't win this duet/duel with MJ, artistically or otherwise, and pulled out. I also think that Prince left the project because he thought Michael wasn't making the song dark enough. To Prince's credit, when he left the studio he turned and said to us, "It will be a big hit, even if I am not on it!"

After a while Michael wrote the incredible lyric for "Bad," and the project and the title song, were then known as "Bad." The video for the song was directed by Martin Scorsese and featured an appearance by a then-unknown Wesley Snipes. "Bad" was one of five number-one hit singles from the album of the same name.

I think Quincy's "casting" of the band was brilliant, with Jimmy Smith, the jazz organist, playing the Hammond B-3 and the MIDI organ solo. Michael does a great little mouth percussion part on "Bad" that I call "How Now Brown Cow."

It's interesting to me to reflect on the album *Bad*, and realize that I have more favorite songs on this album than any of the other M. J. albums. Many people have told me that the sound on the *Bad* album is the best of all the Michael Jackson albums. I don't know about that.

Westlake Studio D on Santa Monica Boulevard—the recording room.

THE *BAD* TOUR GOES TO JAPAN

To kick off Michael's *Bad* tour, it was decided that all of crew would fly to Japan together. Happily, Bea and I were included. For this, we had a huge Boeing 747 jumbo jet. Quincy was there with his latest lady, Christine. They fought throughout the entire trip. While we were waiting for our flight in the VIP lounge at LAX, a courier who brought us a tape from Stevie Wonder met us. It was addressed to me. It was a 24-track tape of a song that Michael was going to sing on for a duet with Stevie. Stevie's voice was already on the tape. Michael was to overdub his voice on the tape in Tokyo.

Marlon Brando stopped by to say goodbye to his son Miko Brando, who worked for Michael. We had a great time meeting Marlon. Miko was going along with Michael on the trip, as security, I think. Miko is a fabulous guy! Bea and I love him. The trip was a blast!

When our plane landed at Narita Airport part of the terminal had been closed to all but us and 1500 members of the press. *Big mistake!* When the door of the plane opened, first off the plane were two of Michael's security guards, and then Michael, his manager (at the time) Frank DiLeo, Quincy, Christine, Bea, and then me.

The members of the press had been given small wooden ladders of varying heights to stand on. All 1500 of them! Soon all hell broke loose, as these photographers and reporters, from all over the globe, shoved, pushed, and shouted at Michael. Frank DiLeo yelled out for us to make a circle around Michael, quick! We did! It was total pandemonium. Never have we experienced such rudeness!

"THE SLAM-DUNK SISTERS"

Michael started a wonderful tradition during the recording of *Bad*. Every Friday evening about 5:00 p.m., Michael's cooks from the ranch, Catherine Ballard and Laura Raynor, would come to the studio and cook an absolutely delicious evening meal for the entire studio crew. Eventually, it became "Family Night." Family members and friends of the crew, along with their assorted pets, were included in this happy event.

Michael's cooks were absolutely top-notch culinary experts. Quincy nicknamed them "The Slam-Dunk Sisters" because every dinner they did for us was a winner! We had incredible delicious homemade tomato soup every dinner every Friday evening! Ten-course turkey dinner one Friday! Ten-course meatloaf dinner next Friday! It was incredible! That tradition that Michael started made us feel like a real family. This same tradition continued through the recording of his albums *Dangerous* and *HIStory, Book I*. For some reason (I don't know why) it was discontinued after we completed *HIStory, Book I*.

If I had one overall comment about the sound of *Bad*, I would have to say that this album has the widest variety of soundfields; for instance, the huge-sounding rhythm section on "The Way You Make Me Feel." "The Way You Make Me Feel" is a shuffle rhythm, which makes for a fantastic dance track. "Man in the Mirror" is a popular music masterpiece.

"SPEED DEMON"

The day we were set to record the track for "Speed Demon," I was a little bit late getting started in the morning. I got in my "Big Bronco" Ford truck in Thousand Oaks and headed for the studio in Hollywood. I got on the freeway and I guess I wasn't watching my speedometer. Pretty soon, flashing lights, and sirens! I was in trouble! The next thing I knew, a courteous California cop was writing me a speeding ticket.

She said I was going 80! I hadn't had a speeding ticket for many years, and I haven't had one since! "Speed Demon!" — that's me! Does Michael have a great imagination, or what? "Speed Demon" is amazing.

"THE WAY YOU MAKE ME FEEL"

I was in the studio one day, making a special mix of "The Way You Make Me Feel" for one of my seminars. I took all the band tracks out of the mix, and left in only Michael's lead vocal track, plus his finger snaps track, and a track of Michael's mouth percussion. (Michael is a master at beat-box mouth percussion. He can be an entire rhythm section all by himself!) I thought that way my class could hear all of Michael's beautiful lead vocal, with his dancing sounds intact, and hear how the dancing sounds affect the overall sonic picture. I would hate to record Michael with what I would call the clinical approach. If I were to try to have Michael's sound antiseptically clean, I think it would lose a lot of its earthy charm.

When I was doing that mix, Michael came into the control room and asked me what I was doing. I told him, and he said to me, "It sounds incredible! You should work on that mix just a bit more, and let me hear it." I wondered what he was thinking about. I thought to myself, "What small rhythmic sound would work to enhance this already slammin' track?" I tried the high-hat in the mix with Michael's lead vocal. The danceability of Michael's lead vocal with only the high-hat added was astounding! Wow! What a sound!

Then I had a brainstorm! After a verse and a B section, I put in the vocal background chorus with Michael's big block vocal harmony chorus. That chorus, with all the finger snaps and dancing knocks you right against the wall when it comes in!! I called Michael into the control room and played it for him.

His face lit up, and he started dancing all over the control room! When the music stopped, he said, "Wow! Call Epic Records, and tell them to put your mix out, exactly like this, as a dance record, a club record!" What happened was that Epic Records put out my dance mix of "The Way You Make Me Feel," it went to number one on the Dance Charts in Billboard, and stayed there for three weeks!

Michael asked me to do a dance mix of this fantastic piece of music. I thought this would be a perfect place to try out my then-brand-new Dbx subharmonic generator to trigger a really low note on the down beats. Bea and I were sitting down at home in California having breakfast one Saturday morning, when I got a phone call from Frankfurt, Germany. The owner of a very popular dance club in Frankfurt came on the phone and said, in a thick German accent, "*You owe me eight voofers!*" It seems that one of my huge low notes had knocked out eight of his very expensive sub-woofers onthe first note! That's one of the biggest compliments I ever got!

"LIBERIAN GIRL"

"Liberian Girl" is one of my absolute favorites of all the music that I've done with Michael. Who could think of a thing like that, except Michael Jackson? It's astounding—the imagery, and everything else in it. It's just an amazing musical and sonic fantasy.

I love the intro. Quincy had Leta M'Bulu say, "Naku penda piya—naku taka piya—mpenziwe," in Zulu, in the intro and in every turnaround. I think that sexy, little speaking line gave the "Liberian Girl" an identity in this wonderful song. Really nice. Michael's vocals on "Liberian Girl" are absolutely stellar! The lead, and the big, block background harmonies. Wow!

UNDER THE MICROSCOPE:"BAD" AND "MAN IN THE MIRROR"
Bad Album. Released August 28, 1987. It is the first album in the history of recorded music to have five consecutive #1 pop hits by a single artist.

MUSIC

"Bad" — 4:06
  Written and composed by Michael Jackson

Musicians:
  Michael Jackson: Solo and background vocals
  Percussion: How Now Brown Cow
  Jimmy Smith: Hammond B3 MIDI organ solo
  Greg Phillinganes: Synthesizer solo
  John Robinson: Drums
  David Williams: Guitar
  Kim Hutchcroft, Larry Williams: Saxophones
  Gary Grant, Jerry Hey: Trumpets
  Paulinho da Costa: Percussion
  Christopher Currell: Synclavier keyboards, digital guitar, rubba
  John Barnes, Michael Boddicker, and Greg Phillinganes: Synthesizers

  Rhythm arrangement by Michael Jackson, Christopher Currell, and
    Quincy Jones
  Horn arrangement by Jerry Hey
  Vocal arrangement by Michael Jackson
  Vocal consultant: Seth Riggs

"Man in the Mirror" — 5:18
  By Siedah Garrett and Glen Ballard

WHAT IS THE "EFFECT" ON THE CHOIR IN "MAN IN THE MIRROR"?

As far as I'm concerned, the song "Man in the Mirror" is the centerpiece, musically speaking, of the Michael Jackson album *Bad*. I recorded the Andrae Crouch choir on "Man in the Mirror" with only two microphones. I used my favorite pair of Neumann M-49s in the classic "Blumlein Pair" method, one of my unquestionably favorite true, stereophonic microphone techniques. This is perhaps the best known of all single-point stereo microphone techniques.

"Blumlein Pair" is the name for the stereo recording technique invented by Alan Dower Blumlein for the creation of recordings that—upon replaying—recreate the spatial characteristics of the original recorded signal. The pair consists of an array of two matched microphones of bi-directional (figure 8) pickup pattern, positioned 90° from each other. The microphone capsules are placed as close to each other as physically possible. The Blumlein pair produces an exceptionally realistic stereo image, but the quality of recordings is highly dependent on the acoustics of the room

In my lectures and seminars around the world, I have often been asked, "What is the effect that you used on the choir on 'Man in the Mirror'?" Isn't that something? There is *no* effect on the choir on "Man in the Mirror." I try to explain that fact by saying that the recording of the choir on "Man in the Mirror" is a classic (but simple) stereo microphone technique! Of course, in addition, you have the best gospel choir in the world, in one of the best studios in the world (Westlake Audio's gorgeous Studio D, in Hollywood)! I did put a squirt of high-quality reverb from my EMT 250 on the choir. But not much!

This wonderful piece of music has a graceful, natural sounding, dynamic curve to it. From the transparent, burnished brass synthesized bells in the intro, to the Andrae Crouch choir that comes in at the modulation. And, of course, the music climaxes with the huge ending.

Musicians:
> Michael Jackson: Solo and background vocals
> Ollie E. Brown: Clap
> Dan Huff: Guitar
> Greg Phillinganes: Keyboards
> Glen Ballard, Randy Kerber: Synthesizers

Background vocals:
> Siedah Garrett; The Winans: Carvin, Marvin, Michael, and Ronald Winans; and Andrae Crouch and the Andrae Crouch Choir: Sandra Crouch, Maxi Anderson, Rose Banks, Geary Faggett, Vonceile Faggett, Andrew Gouche, Linda Green, Franche Howard, Jean Johnson, Perry Morgan, and Alfie Silas

Rhythm arrangement by Glen Ballard and Quincy Jones
Synthesizer arrangement by Glen Ballard, Quincy Jones, and Jerry Hey
Vocal arrangement by Andrae Crouch

The shower at Westlake Studio D, a room that found itself being put to good use during the recording of *Bad*. Handclaps were recorded in this room, and if you listen closely to the album, you might hear the character that this small room lent to the recording—the short delay and the echo produced in that room did lend itself very well to the recording as a whole. So even if that was not the intended use of that particular room, it did indeed come in handy during the recording of *Bad*.

DANGEROUS

When Michael and I began work on the *Dangerous* album, we were recording at Larrabee North Studios in Hollywood. As usual, we had run over the deadline required by the record label. So Michael, Bea, and I moved to the Hilton Universal City Hotel to be near the studio. Staying at the Hilton, in the morning all we would have to do was have Bea take Michael down the service elevator and through the kitchen. Then we would get in my Big Bronco and go to the studio.

One night, or I should say morning, we returned to the hotel at 3:00 a.m. only to discover that Michael had misplaced his room key. So we all went to my room. Bea called the front desk and asked for a replacement key for Mr. Sherman. Now try to get a room key to the room registered to "Mr. Sherman" (Michael's code name at the time), at 3:00 a.m. When we called the front desk, we were told that there was no one in the hotel that could authorize this. We suggested that perhaps they could send up a cot. (No response from the hotel night manager.) Well, we sat around with Michael and had a great time joking and telling crazy stories. Finally, the night manager arrived with a key for Michael for his room.

Here's a question that I am asked from time to time: "Bruce, what is it that you do in the studio?" I always answer, "I do anything in the studio that they'll let me do!" That means that I record music, I mix music, I compose music, and I arrange music. *However*, when I say that "I compose music" or that "I arrange music," I know that I have worked with the best that the industry has to offer. I am embarrassed to say that I do not fit in with those incredible artists. I do what I do and I'd like to leave it like that.

"JAM"

The following little story perfectly illustrates what I mean when I say, "I'll do anything in the music recording studio that they'll let me do!" My studio pal Rene Moore and I composed and recorded a piece of music for Rene's album on Motown Records. Rene and I have composed the music for and produced several projects together.

We had been experimenting with the "looping" of old, but extremely high-energy drum and rhythm tracks. Now, that is a great idea, but many recording people have been doing exactly that for quite some time. However, our idea was to take the fantastic feel of these vintage drum performances, and then layer them with new, very contemporary sounds on parallel tracks to bring the sonic value of the groove up to date. We worked on one of these ideas for some time to on a song to use on Rene's own album on Motown Records. I even used some sleigh bells from my grandfather's farm in Minnesota, as a rhythm element!

The song was really beginning to shape up, and one afternoon we both looked at each other and Rene said, "Maybe we had better play this one for Michael!" We did, and Michael absolutely loved the concept! That was how "Jam" from the Michael Jackson album *Dangerous* came to life. "Jam" was composed by Rene Moore, Bruce Swedien, Michael Jackson, and Teddy Riley.

THE NORWEGIAN SHERPA

Early one morning, my good friend Trond Braaten called me from Fredrikstad, Norway and said that in a week he would be coming to the U.S. and he was going to hand-carry, on the plane, a very heavy Norwegian-made power amplifier that was going to change my life! I thought to myself, "Yeah, sure." Up to that point in time, all I knew about Norway could be summed up in these words: "beautiful boats and *salmon*!" I learned something that day. Don't ever underestimate the Norwegians!

Trond arrived on my doorstep, huffing and puffing, carrying an obviously extremely heavy box. They don't call Trond Braaten the Norwegian Sherpa for nothing! (Sherpa means mountain-climber from northern India, able to carry very heavy objects great distances.) That heavy box contained a power amplifier that did change my life! I stared at the lettering on the box, and thought, "Electrocompaniet, holy cow! What a name! Almost impossible to pronounce. These amplifiers had better be really good!"

We hooked up the amplifier to my speakers. Wow! Great sound! Trond was right; my studio life has not been the same since; those wonderfully musical sounding amplifiers go with me to every recording project.

UNDER THE MICROSCOPE: "JAM" AND "KEEP THE FAITH"

Dangerous Album. Released November 22, 1991.

ED'S NOTE: Bruce Swedien co-composed "Jam," co-produced five songs, and recorded and mixed eleven songs.

> Recorded, mixed and mastered with the exclusive "Quantum Range Recording Process."
> Executive producer: Michael Jackson
> Recorded and mixed by Bruce Swedien, Teddy Riley, and Bill Botrell
> Technical directors: Brad Sundberg and Thom Russo.
> Assistant Engineers: Brad Sundberg, Bart Stevens, Thom Russo, John Chamberlin, Rail Ragut, Dan Bosworth, Julie Last, and Elaine Anderson
> Vocal consultant: Seth Riggs
> Recorded and mixed at Ocean Way Studios, Los Angeles; Record One Studios, Los Angeles; and Larrabee Studios, Los Angeles
> Album production coordinators: Ivy Skoff, Laura Grovner, Nina Greenfield, David Friend, David Nordahl, and Kathryn Litsas
> Thanks to: Bea Anderson-Swedien, Tommy Mottola, and Larry Stessel
> Additional recording at Westlake Audio, Los Angeles; Ocean Way Studios, Los Angeles; Smoketree Studios, Chatsworth; Toad Hall, Pasadena; and The Record Plant, Los Angeles

Special thanks to the Ocean Way, Record One staff: Allen Sides, Claris Sayadian, Mike Wambsgans, Ron Soloman, Garry Creiman, Patty Metroulas, Laurie Rox, Lotti Keirkegaard, Noel Hazen, Rob Disner, and Richard Veltrop

Special thanks to the Larrabee Studio staff: Kevin Mills, Bruce "Desk Doctor" Millett, Chris Behr, Will Williams, Kymee O'Donnell, Maura Gallagher, Jazman, Bill Kaylor, Stephen Pyle, Marko Fox, Reggie Williams, Jamie Romero, and Janet Robin.

Recorded, mixed and mastered with Monster Cable

Special thanks to Brüel and Kjaer Microphones, Mats Holm of Milab Microphones, and Sam Spinnachio of Klark-Teknik Research, LTD

Special thanks to the Slam-Dunk Sisters: Catherine Ballard and Laura Raynor

Mastered by Bernie Grundman at Bernie Grundman Mastering in Los Angeles, Wednesday October 30, 1991

MUSIC

"Jam" — 5:39

Music by Rene Moore, Bruce Swedien, Michael Jackson, and Teddy Riley
Song and lyrics by Michael Jackson
Produced by Michael Jackson, Teddy Riley, and Bruce Swedien.

Michael Jackson: Solo and background vocals
Arrangement by: Michael Jackson, Bruce Swedien, Teddy Riley, and Rene Moore.
Vocal arrangement by Michael Jackson
Rap performance by Heavy D
Rene Moore, Teddy Riley, Bruce Swedien, and Brad Buxer: Keyboards
Teddy Riley and Rhett Lawrence: Synthesizers.
Michael Boddicker and Brad Buxer: Synthesizers
Teddy Riley and Bruce Swedien: Drums
Teddy Riley: Guitar

"Keep the Faith" — 5:57

Written and composed by Glen Ballard, Siedah Garrett, and Michael Jackson
Produced by Michael Jackson; co-produced by Bruce Swedien
Recorded and mixed by Bruce Swedien

Michael Jackson: Solo and background vocals

Arrangement by: Glen Ballard, Jerry Hey, and Rhett Lawrence
Choir arrangement by Andrae and Sandra Crouch, Featuring the Andrae
  Crouch Singers
Background vocals: Siedah Garrett and Shanice Wilson
Jai Winding: Piano and bass
Rhett Lawrence: Drums, percussion, and synthesizers
Bruce Swedien: Drums and percussion
Michael Boddicker: Synthesizers
David Williams: Guitar

The Grammy Award that we earned for the work done on *Dangerous*.

HIStory

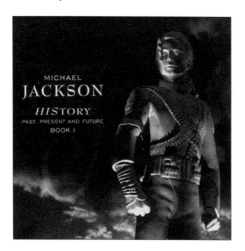

I will always sacrifice a technical value for a production value. In other words, to me there is no technical rule, axiom, or creed that is so sacred as to make itself more important than a musical value, or production value, in the recording of modern music.

If I were looking for a very breathy, sensuous, vocal recording sonic image, for instance, I would place the singer as close as is physically possible to the microphone, thereby eliminating almost all early reflections. If possible, I would even use no windscreen. You can hear this technique in action for yourself, as I used it on Michael Jackson's lead vocal on "Earth Song" from Michael's *HIStory* album. I recorded Michael's lead vocal on "Earth Song" with one of my Neumann M-49 tube mics. I used no windscreen. I placed him as close as he could possibly get to this incredible old mic. "Earth Song" is a piece of music that has many different effects and reverbs as part of its sonic image.

Since right now we are discussing mainly a vocal sound, I'd like to take this opportunity to point out that I came up with a very unusual Lexicon 224XL "Inverse Room"-type lead vocal effect for my mix of "Earth Song." As an additional point of interest, there is a highly modified TC Electronics M5000 "Wooden Hall" reverb on the drums.

When we did Michael's song "Have You Seen My Childhood?" and the Charlie Chaplin song "Smile" on the *HIStory* album, Michael sang live with the orchestra. We recorded both songs in one session at the Hit Factory in New York. Those live vocal takes are mainly what we used to finish both songs; I think Michael punched in a line or two on both songs. His live vocals were so fantastic! You can listen for yourself to those two songs on *HIStory*. That's all the fixing that he made on either song,

For recording a large orchestra in a large studio my preferred microphone technique is, of course, based on a Decca Tree microphone system. I have used the Decca Tree mic system for many years. I simply love it for this application! I would characterize the Decca Tree system as a classic microphone placement system. It is actually an elaborate, beautifully designed, and manufactured microphone stand. Here's how it works.

The Decca Tree is a technique of recording that grew out of Decca's research and development into stereo, which started in 1954. The first Decca stereo products (60 records and four reproducers) came in 1958. Decca Records has a long tradition of developing their own methods and technology, and so they set out to develop their own method of recording stereo as well as developing their own proprietary designs of mixing consoles and other recording equipment. The use of the three-microphone technique that has come to be known as the "Decca Tree" grew out of the desire to maximize the clarity and depth of opera and orchestral recordings.

The actual "tree" is a triangle of microphones, placed roughly ten to twelve feet above the stage level, above and just behind the conductor and arranged on a specially designed and constructed microphone stand. The orchestra's image is adjusted so that the center mic goes equally to both left and right channels of the stereo buss. The right tree mic goes to the right stereo buss, and the left tree mic to the left stereo buss. When this technique was first used in 1954, the microphones used were Neumann KM 56s, tilted 30 degrees toward the orchestra. Other microphones were tried, including the cardioid M-49 (in baffles), in 1955. Soloists with the orchestra were usually spot miked.

The use of the tree has remained virtually unchanged since the '60s, although Decca engineers have made minor modifications to the microphone placement on the tree. In a typical Decca recording session, every effort is taken to find a suitable recording venue with desired reverberation characteristics. As for the spacing of the three mics themselves, this varies with the venue used and with the size of the ensemble. The size of the triangle itself varies with the amount of width and spaciousness desired. Here I am adjusting one of the "sweetener" mics that I placed in the orchestra to bring out a part.

When Michael and I were working on his *HIStory* album at the Hit Factory in New York in 1994, he called me into his rooms at the studio one day, and asked me if I could think of anyone that I had ever worked with in the studio who was truly original in the crafting of synthesizer sounds and colors. Michael added, "And I mean *truly* original." I said to Michael, "Well there's Chuck Wild, of Missing Persons. He *is* indeed original. His sounds are the greatest!" I had worked with the band Missing Persons in 1984 on their wonderful album *Rhyme and Reason*. Fantastic experience! While on that project I met Chuck Wild, who was the synthesizer player with Missing Persons. I called Chuck at his home in Los Angeles and asked him if he would make some of his marvelous synth sounds for Michael on the new *HIStory* album.

Here's what it looks like. Hit Factory/ Criteria—Decca-Tree Microphone System. (2001)—empty studio.

Adjusting a U-87 in the cello section. (2001)

UNDER THE MICROSCOPE: "EARTH SONG" AND "SMILE"

HIStory: Past, Present, and Future. Released June, 1995.

ED'S NOTE: Bruce Swedien composed "2 BAD" and "This Time Around," co-produced three songs, and recorded and mixed 28 songs.

MUSIC

"Earth Song" — 6:45
> Written and composed by Michael Jackson
> Produced by Michael Jackson for MJJ Productions and David Foster for
> Chartmaker Productions
> Co-produced by Bill Botrell
> Recorded and mixed by Bruce Swedien
>
> Michael Jackson: Solo and Background Vocals
> Piano by David Paich

"Smile" — 4:55
> (A tribute to Charlie Chaplin taken from the stage version of "Smile")
> Words by John Turner and Geoffrey Parsons
> Music composed by Charles Chaplin
> Produced by David Foster for Chartmaker, Inc. and Michael Jackson for
> MJJ Productions

I'd like to discuss a piece of music that will illustrate a very unique mixing and balancing assignment. It is "Smile," the Charlie Chaplin composition performed by Michael Jackson. We recorded "Smile" March 29, 1995 at the Hit Factory studios in New York. It is a recording and mixing situation that I have had a bit of experience with over the years, so conveying the beauty of this lovely music, to the eventual listener, was right up my alley. This piece of music was played by a large orchestra, mainly strings, with vocal.

Part of the music, but more or less incidental, is a rhythm section, mainly electronic, with synthesizer parts and colors that have been overdubbed. To me, when recording a piece of music of this style, the mixing concept actually begins before the conductor's down beat. Here's the way it works (for me anyway).

First, I looked over the arrangement, and discussed the studio setup with Jeremy Lubbock, the arranger. I decided to set up the orchestra (in the studio) with the physical positioning of the instruments clearly in mind. In other words, the positioning of the instruments in the stereo panorama of the final mix is precisely the same as the way I set up the orchestra in the studio for the initial recording. I borrowed a studio setup technique that I used some years back, in Chicago, in Studio A at Universal Recording, when I was recording the strings of the Chicago Symphony Orchestra, performing some Gustav Mahler selections for RCA Victor Red Seal.

Actually, Mahler had noted on the score what the orchestra setup must be for the performance of the music of his we were doing at the time. This is precisely the orchestra setup that I used for "Smile." What makes it different from what we frequently hear in recordings of this type is that the first violins are set up to the left of the conductor, and the second violins are set up to the right of the conductor. The violas are just behind the first violins and the celli are behind the second fiddles. The basses are in the rear, more or less in the middle. I did indulge myself a bit when it came to the harps. Jeremy wrote the harp part to be performed by two harps, so I placed the harps far left and right to add a bit of left-right intensity interest in the mix.

The studio I selected for this recording was the large music studio at the Hit Factory in New York. In some recordings of this type, I would have chosen to record the orchestra in a concert hall to give the music the acoustical ambience of true concert orchestra reality. However, since this piece is rather pop music in concept, I figured that a large music studio would be the place to realize this piece.

To check for good "presence" on each part of the arrangement, the best way I have come up with to do that is when the string section has assembled and is ready to start, have each player play the same pitch (note) separately. Listen in the control room to make sure that each player sounds equally present. You can then make individual adjustments by moving a player closer to the mic if he sounds too far away or have him move back a bit if he sounds too close. With a little practice, you can ask the entire string section to play a chord, and when you hear all the notes in the chord with equal presence, you will have a good balance.

Both of the above methods are very simplistic in approach and will give a fairly good balance but not a great string sound. There is much more involved in getting a superb string sound than just getting equal volume level and presence on all parts. My favorite way to balance a string section (and to my ear the most satisfying) is to have a conductor's part in the control room with me that has all the notes of the string parts on it, including all harmony and counter-melodies indicated, etc.

I will ask the string section to rehearse the part, including all the dynamics that are indicated, and as I read the string parts on the conductor's sketch, I visualize each part in my mind's ear and make sure that each part has equal presence and dynamic level. To me, this is the best way to balance a string section, because this method takes into account the dynamic differences that occur in the different registers that the parts are being played in.

It has always seemed to me that a good string section should be miked and recorded in almost the same way you would mic and record a fine choir. There often is, to my ear, a definite sonic similarity between these two musical sound sources. I normally record a string section on two or more channels of the multitrack tape. These two channels are panned hard left and hard right in the monitor speakers. During the recording, the violins are panned full left, the violas center but slightly to the right, and the celli are panned from center to right.

When we finished recording "Have You Seen My Childhood?" and the Charlie Chaplin song "Smile" with the orchestra, Michael asked me if he could go out in the studio and meet the musicians in the orchestra. On the studio talkback I asked Jeremy Lubbock (arranger and conductor) if Michael could come out and meet the orchestra. Of course, he said "Absolutely!" During the recording, the entire orchestra had been listening to Michael sing through their individual headphones. When Michael walked out in the studio to meet then orchestra, the orchestra gave him a standing ovation! Every member of the 50-piece orchestra stood up and tapped their music stands with their bows, as loud as they could! Jeremy stood on the conductor's podium and also applauded as loud as he could! I was applauding, by myself in the control room as loud as I could! Michael was thrilled!

> Michael Jackson: Solo vocal
> Orchestra arranged and conducted by Jeremy Lubbock
> Recorded and mixed by Bruce Swedien
> Vocal Consultant: Seth Riggs
> David Paitch on keyboards

ORCHESTRA SETUP FOR "SMILE" AS RECORDED FOR *HIStory*

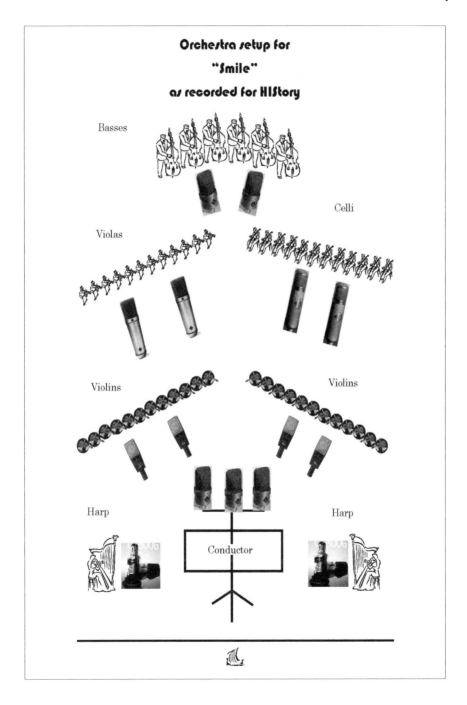

INVINCIBLE

An important event in my studio life occurred at the same time that I started work on Michael Jackson's *Invincible* album. We were working at the Record Plant Recording Studios recording new rhythm tracks on North Sycamore Avenue in Hollywood. That was the time that I started using Royer ribbon microphones. Of course, the Royer ribbon mic is a very modern version of my beloved classic ribbon mics such as the RCA 44BX and the RCA 77DX.

I have always loved the sound of the ribbon microphone, but now, often a ribbon mic can be my first choice for critical sound sources. I absolutely love my new Royer R-122Vs. Something happened when Royer put that tube into their same proven microphone system. The high operating voltage of the vacuum tube provides a headroom capability far beyond that available from a standard phantom powersupply.

It also provides a sensitivity that is absolutely fantastic! I have a feeling that the sensitivity of the R-122V rivals many of the new condenser mics available today. In studio use, this translates into incredible clarity and detail. In reality, though, it also solves two of the major issues that make it difficult to use a classic ribbon microphone in modern recording. Those two issues, of course, are competitive output level and competitive sensitivity.

I have always used ribbon mics for their unique warmth of sound quality and attractive high frequency response characteristics. However, there is something truly unique about the R-122Vs sound quality that I haven't found in another microphone.

UNDER THE MICROSCOPE:
"SPEECHLESS" AND "WHATEVER HAPPENS"

Invincible Album. Released October 30, 2001.

MUSIC

"Speechless" 3:20
>   Written and composed by Michael Jackson
>   Produced by Michael Jackson
>   Recorded and mixed by Bruce Swedien
>   Arranged by Michael Jackson
>   Michael Jackson: Lead vocal
>   Vocal consultant: Seth Riggs
>   Orchestra arranged and conducted by Michael Jackson and Jeremy
>   Lubbock
>   Keyboards performed by Brad Buxer

> *Andrae Crouch and The Andrae Crouch Singers*: Alfie Silas Durio, Valerie
> Doby, Maxi Anderson, Kristie Murden, Patrice Morris, Yvonne Williams,
> Vonclele Williams, Tenike Johns, Angel Johnson, Linda McCrary, Sue
> Merritt, Deborah Sharp-Taylor, Marja Dozier, Zaneta M. Johnson,
> Gloria Augustus, Alice Jean McRath, Sandra Crouch, Zandra Williams,
> Judy Gossett, Greary Lanier Faggett, Johnnie Walker, Ron Taylor,
> Daniel Johnson, Harold Green, Laquentan Jordan, Tim Brown, Howard
> McCrary, Sam McCrary, Kevin Dorsey, and Andrae Crouch.

> Viola/contractor: Novi Novoq
> Viola: Thomas Tally
> Violins: Peter Kent, Gina Kronstadt, Robin Lorentz, Kirstin Fife, and
>   John Wittenburg
> Digital editing by Brad Buxer and Stuart Brawley

"Whatever Happens" 5:36
>   Written and composed by Michael Jackson
>   Produced by Michael Jackson
>   Recorded and mixed by Bruce Swedien
>   Arranged by Michael Jackson
>   Michael Jackson: Lead vocal

Vocal consultant: Seth Riggs
Orchestra arranged and conducted by Michael Jackson and Jeremy
  Lubbock
Carlos Santana: Guitar

STUDIOS USED FOR THE RECORDING OF MICHAEL'S ALBUMS

The Wiz
  A & R Studios in New York, Studios A1 and R1

Off the Wall
  Cherokee Studios in Hollywood
  Westlake Audio on Wilshire Boulevard
  Allen Zentz in Hollywood

E.T. The Extra Terrestrial (Soundtrack)
  Westlake Audio on Beverly Boulevard

Thriller
  Westlake Audio on Beverly Boulevard

Victory
  Westlake Audio on Beverly Boulevard

Bad
  Westlake Audio on Santa Monica Boulevard
  The Hit Factory in New York

Dangerous
  Larrabee Studios North in North Hollywood

HIStory Volume One
  Record One Studios in Van Nuys
  The Hit Factory in New York

Invincible
  Sony Music Studios in New York
  The Hit Factory in New York
  The Hit Factory/Criteria in Miami

The EMT 250 Electronic Reverberator Unit.

MY RECOLLECTION OF WORKING WITH MICHAEL JACKSON ON *HIStory*
by Chuck Wild

I'll never forget the first conversation Michael and I had in 1994. He said, "Chuck, I want you to manufacture sounds that the human ear has never heard. I want them to be fiery and aggressive, unusual and unique." Michael's instructions raised the bar and changed the way I looked at sound design. Off and on over the next three years, working with about 25 synths, three samplers, and a couple of Macintosh computers, I created a library of sounds and soundscapes. Michael distributed those sounds to others working on HIStory and subsequent albums, including "Blood on the Dance Floor." After I had designed about a third of the sounds, producer Bruce Swedien and Brad (Buxer) moved me to a studio in Hollywood, to work with producer/engineer Harry Maslin to ensure the maximum sonic integrity and clarity of the soundscapes.

From a technical standpoint, I combined "found sounds" (both musical and sound FX) from the environment around Los Angeles with pre-existing, license-free samples and synth-programmed sounds (Synclavier), and then used computer software (Hyperprism and Metasynth) to morph and process this regenerated material in numerous ways to make each sound unique and unrecognizable from its original elements. At that point, I would piece together the new disparate elements into a soundscape using a simple sound design program such as Sound Designer to create a new "base" element altogether. The next step was to use the excellent Digital Performer MIDI/audio program to combine and morph between various sounds. Most importantly, I strove to maintain an emotional and energetic visual component in the soundscapes wherever possible. The work was time-consuming, but I think we came up with some truly unusual aural material.

I'm often asked what it was like to work with Michael the musician and producer. He was very patient and well-focused in our meetings. His vision seemed always clear. I would meet with him at the end of my work day at Record One where he was recording vocals with Bruce; Michael would listen to each individual sound I created and comment in a constructive way on how they might or might not be useful, and what he needed in the future for a particular track.

CHRISTMAS WITH MICHAEL DURING THE *HIStory* ALBUM
by Bea Anderson Swedien

When we were recording Michael's *HIStory* album, it was Christmas time. We were working at the Hit Factory in New York. Michael had as his guest one of his nephews, who had quite recently lost his mother. Since Michael was occupied in the studio, he figured this young boy needed the companionship of kids of his own age. So Michael asked his secretary Evvy to call me and ask if the three young children of the Cardona family could come to New York from their home in Connecticut for a few days visit in New York. Michael had met the Cardona family at our home in California the year before. The Cardonas, Javier and Marciella, worked for us on our little horse ranch in California. They have three great kids, Gabriel, Xavier, and Cytllally. The Cardona family came to New York, and Michael put the entire family up in a first-class hotel.

While they were all in New York, all the kids (Michael's nephew included) were treated to a shopping spree at FAO Schwartz at Michael's expense! Of course the entire outing was safely escorted by Michael's security people. As a crowning Christmas touch, Michael arranged for a Christmas party with an enormous Christmas tree, complete with Santa Claus, in huge Studio One at the Hit Factory! Wonderful food and a great time was had by all!

FUNKY TABLA
by Roberta Swedien

The greatest gift my father ever gave me was a seat next to him in the Chicago recording studio control rooms when I was growing up. As a young classical pianist, I was taken far beyond my conservatory education, watching jazz and R&B sessions; the best in the business doing their best. My dad helped me find out what goes into musical "soul"—no matter what the style. "Good music is good music" said Quincy Jones. I learned that very early on.

The greatest gift my mother ever gave me was India; glorious, fascinating India, my home for the last 15 years and another lesson in "soul." My mother's parents came to India in 1926 and she had an amazing childhood growing up amidst the tribals of Nagaland, near the Burmese border. I came here to teach music and to play the piano, starting out at my mom's alma mater, "Woodstock." I have lived in the foothills of the Himalayas in the north; in the bustling capitol, New Delhi; in Tamil Nadu, near the tip of South India; and in the west, a few hours from Bombay, the cosmopolitan city on the Arabian Sea that is the home of Bollywood. The music in this country is mind-boggling.

The second greatest gift my father ever gave me was the chance to work with Michael Jackson! The first time I met Michael, he was standing in the doorway of Studio Two, at the Hit Factory in New York. I was at the piano, playing the lightning-speed *Gigue* from Bach's *B-Flat Major Partita*. Brad Buxer was my only audience, or so I thought. Finally, looking up I saw Michael and realized he had been standing there, listening. He so enjoyed the surprise on my face; we both burst out laughing. He also enjoyed the Bach. I'll never forget the radiance in his eyes, like they were dancing.

I had come from New Delhi to New York to bring funky tabla grooves to the *HIStory* project. My dad had been inspired by listening to Indian music while waiting for his chicken tikka in a little Indian restaurant in a strip mall in L.A. There were moments of pure Motown in that music, and he had a brainstorm to create loops using the Indian percussion and that soulful energy. Michael loved the idea. So, armed with instruments, dance bells, finger cymbals, CDs, and tapes, I travelled to the other side of the globe to make some music for Michael.

A few hours after the Bach encounter, my dad said, "Come on, let's go talk to Michael!" I gathered up my Indian gear and we went into Michael's room—the space at the Hit Factory that he used for songwriting and meetings. It was just the three of us. Michael was warm and welcoming, soft-spoken and very sincere. Even though the setting was relaxed, he seemed to exude a kind of quiet kinetic energy. It was striking and unforgettable.

I pulled the treasures out of their bags (brown paper, to be exact) and handed them to Michael, one by one. Everything aroused his curiosity and interest, but it was the dance bells that fascinated him. These were a gift to Michael from my dear friend, Harash. They had been worn by dancers in his family and were of the Kathak style of North India, a dance form that tells stories from the great epic poems of Hinduism. The design hasn't changed for hundreds of years: leather straps that buckle around the ankle and calf, hundreds of small, round bells sewn on by hand. These were old and had signs of wear and tear. Michael held these bells in his hands and was quiet. Slowly turning them over and over, he suddenly shook them and smiled. "Thank you," he said softly. Shaking them again, his eyes lit up and he said, "We have to sample these!"

We talked about India. He had long had an interest, having heard my mother's stories of her incredible childhood in Nagaland during the British Raj, and was curious to know about my experiences in modern India. But he was concerned about the problems of the country: poverty, population, education, and health care. Michael asked me to choose some classical piano CDs for him to listen to. I suggested the French Impressionists, in particular the Debussy *Preludes*, exquisite soundscapes with titles like "What the West Wind Saw," "Sunken Cathedral," and "Sounds and Scents Mingle in the Evening Air." He loved the imagery and was anxious to hear the music.

I was teamed up with Scott "You Got It!" Patinsky, a brilliant and energetic young sound design whiz-kid. We turned his funky little studio, Compound Sound, into a "funky tabla loop factory." The room resounded with recordings of Indian drums, vocals, sitar, santoor, shennai, bamboo flute, old "filmi" music, Bollywood, Bhangra, and the folk music of Rajastan, the Punjab, and South India—just to get the vibe going. My funk inspiration came from only two sources: James Brown and the Brothers Johnson.

Once the stage was set in our ears, we got down to the business of actual loop making and worked 14 hours a day, seven days a week. We sampled those magnificent dance bells, the finger cymbals, and all the instruments I had brought from Delhi. Scott put the dance bells onto a keyboard so that I, with Rachmaninoff fingers, could play them. Soulful funk met the history and mystery of India. I gave each loop a name: "Bombay Twilight," "Calcutta Backstreet," "Gandhi's Dream," "Bengal Tiger," and so on. The first DAT was delivered to Michael; he loved it and wanted more. We made more than 20 in all.

I was booked into the studio for two weeks. I came out two months later. Needless to say, this was the experience of a lifetime. The highest standards conceivable permeated every facet of this project. People work like this for Michael because he is an artist who truly inspires.

Pune, Maharashtra, India
December 2006

THE *HIStory* PLAYBACK SESSION— FOR THE LABEL BIGWIGS!
by Bea Anderson Swedien

Michael hates doing playback sessions for a record company. A playback session is a big meeting where we play back the new album mixes for the record company bigwigs. Therefore in the past years when these things were suggested, he just simply would not attend. However, Michael's then managers, Sandy Gallin and Jim Morey, talked Michael into attending the one held for the Sony executives to hear the *HIStory* album for the first time at Larrabee North Studios in Hollywood.

I remember Michael was very reluctant. We were about 30 people, all seated in the main control room at Larrabee North Studios. Michael was there, along with Macaulay Culkin. I was sitting with Michael, Macaulay, Sandy Gallin, and Jim Morey near the rear of the control room. The entire album was played — Michael's incredible music.

The last note sounded. All these geniuses from the record label simply got up and left the studio without saying a word! No applause, no comment, no reaction ——I was absolutely mortified! How can people that are supposed to be in the record business be so dumb?

Sandy Gallin was jumping up and down, and waving his arms and screaming at them, "*Are you all brain dead?*" There were tears in Michael's eyes! Bea, Michael, and I went out to the parking lot and got in my Big Bronco. Michael said to me, "I'll never do this again!"

CHAPTER 2

THE FUTURE OF MUSIC IS IN GOOD HANDS

For those that might wonder were the music industry is going these days, it must be comforting to know that the music at least is in good hands. There have never been so many involved in creating and recording music as there are today, and the quality of both the music and the audio, in a lot of instances, is very high indeed.

In the following part of this book there will be some inserts on how the music recorded by Michael Jackson has affected a few persons from around the world, as well as some examples of fans that have been part of the great success that Michael Jackson's music has seen through these years.

So even if how music is being distributed might be up for a dramatic change, the music is in very good hands indeed, and from the looks of it there will be plenty of opportunities for those that'll make music their living in the time to come—and this should also be good to know for those that enjoy listening to music.

The future of music is in good hands.

Bruce with Keith Henderson in Keith's studio.

RUSS RAGSDALE

It's hard for me to believe that over 20 years have passed since I first met Bruce Swedien, Michael Jackson, and Quincy Jones. I remember specifically thinking in 1987 when I was just beginning my professional career in music, "I wonder what I am going to be doing 20 years from now, just how all of this music will play out." Well I'm here to tell everyone, my career has turned out just fine and I wouldn't change a thing about how it's unfolded. My story is an interesting one; please let me tell you how it all started and how much of a mentor Bruce Swedien has been in my life.

I was bitten by the music bug upon buying my first album, *Meet the Beatles*. At the time I was a pretty shy kid, and when my parents saw how music was affecting me, they bought me an electric guitar and enrolled me into lessons by the second grade. Little did they know that music would be my career of choice. I was never a very good student in school. However, while on a holiday break years later, I discovered that all the report cards included in the childhood memorabilia my mom had saved in her attic had a common thread. The back of every report card had teachers' comments: "If Russ would concentrate on his studies as much as he concentrates on art and music, he'd probably be a pretty good student." Oh, that discovery made me puff my chest out and say "yeah."

In 1982, a friend suggested I get a four-track tape machine, which I did and still have as sort of a memento. It was after writing and recording tons of songs with my friends that I discovered I enjoyed engineering more than being a musician. I could hardly see the carpet on the floor for all of the cables running everywhere, and knew I needed to do something about that. I went directly from my four-track to getting up the courage to knock on the door of a local 24-track studio in my home town of Tyler, Texas. I spent a couple of years helping out with the recording of music primarily used for radio and television commercials. This satisfied me for a while, but I wanted to record real songs, with real artists, and just instinctively knew Los Angeles was where I needed to be.

Here's where my story gets pretty interesting. I knew absolutely no one in Los Angeles; I just knew that this was where I was supposed to be. In 1986 I loaded up my truck and U-Haul and headed west. I'd just figure it out once I got there. I had enough money in my pocket to pay my rent two months in advance (later I found out Michael Jackson owned the apartment I was living in), but after that, I was going to need a job. So I started knocking on studio doors, just cold calling. Fortunately, I found everyone that I talked to, to be very nice and encouraging, which helped me keep my spirits up. After three weeks I started getting several offers. I was feeling pretty good about an interview I'd had with Westlake Audio in Hollywood, and finally my prayers were answered. Westlake Audio thought I'd be an asset to their studios, and Michael Jackson's *Bad* album would end up being my very first gig in L.A.! I swear it wasn't any harder than following a dream, but more importantly putting that dream into action.

The album project had just started, but Michael was in New York shooting the video for "Bad" while work was still in progress at Westlake Studio D. I first met Bruce; then came in Quincy. Very soon after that I met Michael, and for the next two years we rolled up our shirt sleeves and made the most fantastic album that I have ever been involved with, still to this day. It was sink or swim—I was thrown into the deep end of the pool. Luckily I'm a pretty good swimmer. Back then, I didn't even know what questions to ask. It all makes more sense to me now, but man was I ever at the right place to learn. It didn't dawn on me until months after finishing the *Bad* album just how big of piece of history that album would become and how it would be embraced around the world. What a thrill to witness all of these soon-to-be number one songs being crafted track by track.

One of the things I quickly noticed about Bruce's sessions is how he and Quincy get the best performances out of people. I've seen the fear of stepping up to the plate just disappear with an embrace of encouragement. Love is everywhere; everyone is family and truly loved. I think Bruce is well aware of the effect of positive and good influence on raw passion.

One fear of mine was that I knew there'd come a day that it would be just Michael and I in the same room one on one. I'd rehearsed it in the mirror over and over; just what was I going to say to this guy? Well, that day came, and what was probably seconds seemed like a very long time. Catering had arrived at the studio and here Michael and I were standing by ourselves. I was looking at the floor and said to myself, "This is it, this is what I'd been afraid of. I'm going to have to break the ice." I took a big deep breath and raised my head to speak and *wham*—I got hit with a handful of corn. I thought, "Oh no, this is going to be war." I picked up some pickles and threw them at Michael, then he threw something else and it went back and forth for a while. We were laughing so hard (I had to clean it all up later of course), but for three weeks we couldn't look at each other without laughing. What a great way for him to make me feel at ease. Michael really has a great sense of humor; he just loves seeing people do a Three Stooges act and fumble all over themselves. I wish there were more people in the world exactly like Michael Jackson. He is truly one amazing human being.

Although Bruce has a set of rules — "Screw up once and you're out of here" — I've never seen anyone fail him. Bruce is so detail-oriented and the instructions are so specific, it almost makes it impossible to fail. Having said that, Bruce has a special gift of delegating duties to other people in order to make people feel like they are a very much appreciated part of the process. Heck, I think he even pulls the janitor aside and makes him feel like this thing wouldn't even fly if it weren't for his contribution.

The musicianship, textures, orchestration, and drama on a Bruce/Quincy session is undeniably hand-picked from the best of the best. I remember standing next to Stevie Wonder as he laid down the most ripping synth solo I'd ever heard on "Just Good Friends." My jaw just about hit the floor when Stevie said, "Bruce can you just burn that one and give me another?" Just about any other engineer would try to save the first take, but later it dawned on me: with Stevie Wonder at the keyboard, you're going to be in pretty good hands. I once heard someone ask Bruce a question regarding how he would deal with a singer who had the tendency to sing off key a bit, and his response was, "Get a better singer." It's no wonder where Bruce is in his career, with the company he keeps.

I've learned a lot from Bruce about what illusions can be created with music. If I were using a four-track machine, I'd make you believe I was using a 16-track; if I were using a 24-track, I'll create the illusion it's 48 tracks, and so forth. This was also my first exposure to using multiple bass and snare drums in the same piece of music. Everything gets recorded in super duper S T E R E O. At one point during the making of *Bad* (on "Smooth Criminal"), I saw two Mitsubishi 32-track X-850 digital machines, one Studer 24-track, and a one-inch 16-track machine, all synchronized together to play in sync. Bruce's tracks are so well crafted that what he's taught me to do makes the faders feel different, the stereo buss act differently, and the dynamics act differently, and it all translates into smiles on the clients' faces as wide as the Grand Canyon. What an experience.

Bruce has taught me how to trust my own feelings and not pay so much attention to what other people are doing. Copying sounds from records that you like is third- or fourth-hand information by the time you hear the final product. Trust what is in your heart and get out there on the cutting edge, because that is where all the fun is. He's taught me to pay close attention to goosebumps; they do not lie. Often when I'm working at a home studio, I'll just close my eyes and reference back to what that big studio sound was all about. I'll literally transport myself back to Westlake Studio D. I've even been known to get on a plane and go back there just to play my current record I've been working on, just for one last final check.

When it comes to technology, Bruce always reminds me that if you have one microphone, one mic pre, EQ, a pan pot, and a fader, you can make a hit record. One of the most important things Bruce and Quincy have taught me that gets used every day in my life is the importance of a strong melody in a song. Those guys can carve out a melody with just the hi-hat. It's breathtaking. I live in Nashville now, and we use the term "legendary songwriter" pretty loosely around here. If you look at the songs Michael Jackson has written, he redefines just what "legendary" really is all about.

I'm very much looking forward to what is around the next corner. Something big always happens musically to mark the end of each decade. I think it is anybody's ball game. Country music saw all-time peaks in much of the 90s; however, the pop scene is gaining strength once again and the new alternative rock bands are all doing fine. These are exciting times we live in. And Bruce's presence in what I've learned and share with others who are also dedicated toward music will assure every listener of great music and an exciting ride for decades to come.

Nashville

PHIL O'KEEFE

Late in 1982, when *Thriller* was released, I was 20 years old. I had started recording music a few years prior to that; mostly tracking my own songs one part at a time at home and doing projects for various bands I was a member of, or for my friends' bands at local studios. At the time, Pro Tools didn't exist, synths were still fairly new, and MIDI was just about to appear on the scene, but it was the dawn of a renaissance of the whole home recording revolution that had originally been pioneered back in the 1950s by guys like Les Paul and Bruce. Radio was still a vibrant avenue for new music in the early 1980s, and MTV was only a little over a year old. Music was starting to become more stylistically polarized then than it had been in the 1960s and early 1970s—you were either a rocker, or a punk, or into R&B or jazz, and there wasn't a lot of crossover. *Thriller* changed all of that in a very big way. Here was an album that nearly everyone liked and could find something to dig about it; from the funk of "Pretty Young Thing" to the rock of "Beat It," it blended a wide range of styles and genres in a very natural and unforced way. It's hard to over-emphasize just how huge it was at the time, and the impact that it had.

Beyond the musical elements that are essential for a great record—the solid, hook-laden songwriting, the masterful arrangements and the skintight grooves and performances—I think the thing that impressed me the most was that melding of influences, emotions, tastes, and intuition into a unique, individual, and personal recording style/voice—what I later learned Bruce refers to as a "sonic personality." *Thriller* bears the unmistakable stamp of Bruce's sonic signature. To me, some of the elements of Bruce's signature include:

Clarity: You can easily pick out each part in the mix.

Stereo soundfield: There is a great sense of depth and space; not only left to right, but from front to back. Bruce is a master of using not only reverbs but early reflections—even on synths —to give a sense of space, placement, and depth to the mix.

The bottom end: *Huge* but *clear!* There's no mud, no mushy mess; just clear, tight, and full foundational support of the tracks from the bottom up, with clear definition between the kick drum and the bass. That foundation has to be there in order to build and support a track, and on *Thriller*, like all of Bruce's mixes, it certainly is.

Emotional impact of the mixes: The tonal and mix decisions Bruce made support and enhance the emotional context of the music, making the impact even stronger. It's not just a collection of gimmicks and tricks thrown in to impress us with the engineer's skills, but instead those techniques and tools are used in a way that is never obtrusive or inappropriate, but always in support of the musical content.

Thriller reset the musical and sonic bar to just incredible heights, and nearly 25 years later, in many ways, that standard has yet to be equaled, yet alone exceeded. It's impossible to be an educated modern musician, producer, or engineer without being influenced by it in some fundamental way. For me, it inspired me and made me realize just what was possible sonically when you combined great songs, killer performances, and an engineer who approached the recording and mixing of an album not just from a clinical and technical standpoint, but from an emotional and artistic point of view. It is that concept of "engineer as sympathetic co-artist" that has probably had the most lasting effect and influence on the way I approach working in the studio, and it is the legacy that Bruce has passed on to all who would attempt to follow in his footsteps.

In my work since then, I have had the good fortune to be able to do what I love for a living—making music. Over the years, I've had the privilege of meeting many influential and successful producers and engineers, and out of all of them, I have never met one who was more interested in "passing it on" to the next generation of cats than Bruce. Unlike some engineers, who jealously guard their hard-earned knowledge and techniques, Bruce has no secrets, and he is actively involved with sharing his experiences and knowledge to those who are just learning the art and craft of making records—ensuring that his legacy will not rest only on his own incredible discography, but also echo on through the work of the people who have learned about the art of recording directly from him.

I consider it a great honor to be among those people, and it is a debt I shall always remember. The responsibility to emulate his example, to pass along the knowledge and love for the art of making records that he passed on to me, is one that I take very seriously. As Bruce is fond of saying, it's about music first—pass it on.

Phil O'Keefe in his own studio.

MARTIN KANTOLA

Little did I expect that my life would change forever when I joined the Bruce Swedien master class at the Sibelius Academy in Helsinki in 1992. Yes, the tracks he played with Michael Jackson blew all of us away (almost literally, may I add), but it was not until I realized the importance of the sonic personality behind these chart-topping recordings and mixes that I felt my own professional career taking a giant leap into a whole new dimension.

Meeting Bruce in person and hearing him talk about how he carefully structured the music, building almost exclusively on his own sensitivity, visions, taste, and reactions, gave music mixing and recording a whole new meaning for me. Almost anybody can build a simple hut, but the sonic equivalent of a palace or castle takes much more planning and dedication. I've learned that one really has to be emotionally involved, or rather, *immersed* in the music to become comfortable enough to work this intimately with the track or project. So nowadays, every time I'm presented with a new project, I sit back and let the music talk to me, and seduce me, hopefully. Not forgetting, but on the contrary, absorbing enough technical knowledge so that I can work more freely and focus on the essential; the music itself! How inspiring to hear directly from Bruce that it was not the equipment, the budgets, or the number of tracks that were behind the magic. Because that meant that the door to this fantastic world of sound was wide open for me too!

When I think of any of these classic songs and masterpieces in audio engineering, I want to compare them to one of those huge paintings I've seen at the famous Louvre museum in Paris. These mixes, these true works of art, have been experienced, loved, and admired by millions and millions of people. Yet, every time I humbly stand before them, I'm more impressed by the quality of the work itself than the numbers of fans. The detail, the depth and large selection of different interesting textures are amazing, but it's when I take a step back and enjoy the big picture that the genius of Bruce's work really strike me. He manages to paint these huge sonic landscapes without losing the important intimacy, personality, and warmth.

There are always a number of contrasts; dramatic juxtapositions between low and high, soft and loud, and even smooth and rough—all of this in one mix, and still you are always able to just sit back and relax and enjoy a great piece of music, letting the emotions of the music so skillfully captured in the recording flow through your whole body, and be transported to another world by the sheer power of it.

One of the many things Bruce has taught me is that everything is important, but also that I can really have it all in the end, if I only set my mind to it, and if I'm ready to work as hard as needed. No free lunches. But the moment I realized that it's all out there, just waiting for me to come and get it, there was no turning back. How exciting to think that I could keep expanding the limits of music recording, not only on a personal level, but perhaps even on a larger scale. And to be perfectly honest, I feels like that's already happening for me, but that's not for me to judge, of course.

Bruce has without doubt been the single most important person in my career. Apart from his unique gift, I think his ability, and most of all his will to share his views, are the main reasons for this. There might be others out there with a similar gift and level of dedication, but I've never met anyone so generous and well spoken in the whole industry. And I have yet to hear anyone record and mix like he does. His work always stands out, as if protected by some magic spell, completely unaffected by time. As I, from time to time, play one of his mixes for sheer inspiration, they impress me just as much, every single time.

His direct and indirect influence has affected and carried me through many years, and continues to do so. One of the key elements I've learned to consider and respect is dynamics, and the many faces it has. It might be that our media and format has very a limited dynamic range sometimes, but that doesn't change the fact that dynamics are such an important part of the magic language of music.

It might sound silly, but I firmly believe that asking myself time after time, "Wonder what Bruce would have done with this?" has made me a better sound engineer. Still, it's definitely not about copying his style of working, or learning all his secret tricks, because to begin with this great man doesn't believe in secrets. And besides, what I think he's trying to teach is to work from your own feelings and gut reactions, creating your own set of references and personal style. It has to flow from me and through me. And that philosophy makes perfect sense to me now, because music is always a highly personal and subjective experience.

Martin Kantola is from Finland, the home of Santa Claus, and he is involved with the group Gjallarhorn, which he recorded and mixed together with Bruce Swedien. He has also designed a variation on the Neumann U-47, called the NU-47. Bruce has one, Björk has another, and the third one is owned by Martin Kantola. Martin Kantola has been the exclusive Gjallarhorn live performance and studio recording sound engineer since their formation and has recorded, mixed, and mastered all of their CDs. He has built microphones for their acoustic instruments as well as tube condenser microphones for vocalists, used by Jenny in Gjallarhorn studio sessions. Martin is also a celebrated inventor and developer of high-end loudspeakers and audio recording equipment, including groundbreaking development of Surround microphones.

Martin Kantola with
me at Westviking
in Florida.

KEITH HENDERSON

My first major music memory is of when my brother, sister, and I went to an all-night-skate at a local roller rink and stayed up until midnight to watch an MTV world premiere of Michael Jackson's "Thriller." At that time, I was only five years old, but that was the start of my admiration of Michael Jackson and his music.

MEETING BRUCE

A few years ago, I received a phone call from a good friend of mine who was the manager of a band that I had recorded a demo for earlier that year. He told me that the band was offered a chance to do some recording with the guy who had produced all the Michael Jackson records. I, of course, was very familiar with all of Michael's work, but had only read of his engineer in books. They wanted to redo a couple of the songs off the demo and needed me to bring over my hard drive so they could use the original session files, so I was off to the studio. I arrived at a horse farm on the outskirts of our small Florida town and was led to a large metal building on the back of the property. When I first walked in, I was kind of shocked not to see a studio, but a room full of farm equipment. It wasn't until we entered the next door that I realized I was truly in the presence of greatness. Through this humble door was a hallway lined with gold and platinum albums for such artists as George Benson, Donna Summers, Quincy Jones, Duke Ellington, Ella Fitzgerald, and of course, Michael Jackson. I think the band and I must have wandered through this museum for at least an hour, studying the many great albums created by the engineer down the hall. After hooking my hard drive into the system, I sat down in the control room and proceeded to load the sessions into the system. This night was one of the most memorable of my career because it was the first time I ever had the honor and privilege to work with one of the greatest producers, engineers, and all around nice guys in the world, my mentor, Bruce Swedien.

The months following that first meeting, Bruce and I spent a lot of time in the studio together. The countless stories and songs I got to hear were amazing. I must have asked him a billion and one questions; "How did you get that sound? What mic did you use on that song? Why is your board so old?" I'm sure I drove him insane, but Bruce, being the great teacher he is, never tired of my long-winded babble. He truly believed in making great records and putting the music first. One of Bruce's most interesting philosophies is "no secrets."

To my surprise, we have a lot in common in the way we record. One of the most important similarities was that we both liked to rely on and use our ears. Trying to recreate what you hear can be very simple, but sometimes people, engineers, and artists try to make everything way too technical. He also showed me that it was okay to take my time. In my young career, I had always been forced to adhere to a strict schedule; the faster I was, the better I was. I learned that this wasn't true at all. I remember Bruce letting me hear recordings of him and Michael in the studio experimenting with different mics, trying multiple effects patches, doing take after take until it wasn't just good enough, but until it was nothing but perfect. After hearing Bruce's approach to recording music, mixing, and doing things until they are right, I realized why so many of us strive to recreate the overall sound, character, and feel that he was able to capture on all of those Michael Jackson albums.

Bruce teaches a lot about developing your own sonic personality. He tells stories about listening to choirs and orchestras in a live setting during his youth. This is something that he says helped develop his sonic personality. So many young engineers and producers have been taught or led to believe that the music they hear on the radio or on CDs is what music should sound like, when, in fact, it is just someone else's opinion of what that music should sound like. Bruce helped teach me that I should always make my sound mine. Even when a client wants a particular artist's sound, I always try to put my twist on it.

I would like to tell two of my favorite stories, or should I say, experiences with Bruce involving Michael Jackson. The first: my entire career in recording has been strictly digital. I am definitely of the computer generation. In the digital world I live in, crisp, clean, noiseless tracks are a way of life. Bruce is always getting on me about cleaning tracks and trying to make things perfect. He says those little noises and imperfections can sometimes make a song. He told me a story about Michael in the studio that illustrated this perfectly. Bruce said that Michael was always dancing. Even while tracking vocals, he always kept a beat with his feet. So, as the old saying goes, "If you can't beat 'em, join 'em." Bruce had a piece of wood brought into the studio for Michael to stand on while he sang. A mic was placed on MJ's feet; what a great idea!

The second story took place after Bruce and I were in his studio working on some music. Just before leaving for the day, he gave me a collection of Michael Jackson CDs as a gift. On my drive home, I put in the *Thriller* album and suddenly, it hit me like a ton of bricks. As I drove and listened to songs like "Thriller," "Beat It," "Bad," "Smooth Criminal," and my favorite, "Man in the Mirror," I realized how blessed I was to be in the position of having my career guided by a legend. To Bruce I will always be thankful.

Rust Productions
Ocala, Florida

Keith Henderson is one of a new breed of sound engineers and producers that's coming up these days. From his private studio, positioned within his music store in Ocala, Florida, he works with various local artists and others.

Keith Henderson
in his Ocala studio.

ARJAN "BOOSH" BOES

When someone asks me what I think of Michael Jackson's *Thriller*, I always flash back to the first time I listened to that album. Imagine this: You close your eyes and a door opens. You enter that door and a whole new world unfolds and starts taking shape. The most wonderful sounds start emerging from nothing, and as if in a dream, you can walk around through sonic soundscapes. It's like feeling, breathing, and hearing in color, from the reddish brown bass line in "Billie Jean" to the golden vocals in "P.Y.T.," all the way across the green slopes of the choir in "Wanna Be Startin' Something" right down to blue sky harmonies of "The Girl Is Mine." That is the experience I had when I put *Thriller* on the turntable the first time.

I remember that day as if it were yesterday. I was 11 years old and a bit of a weird kid. Other kids my age were listening to Top 40 stuff, while I played my father's records. There's no one in my whole family who is interested in music, which is why I'm still amazed when I think of my father's record collection. We had Elvis, Mahalia Jackson, The Beatles, Bill Haley, Ray Charles, Dizzy Gillespie, Gene Krupa, etc., etc. Man, did my dad have some awesome records!

Anyway, of course I had seen the "Beat It" video on TV, but this experience was totally different from actually listening to the entire album. I was sitting in my room listening to "Sh-Boom," recorded by the Crew Cuts in 1954, when my dad walked in and handed me a fresh copy of *Thriller*. That moment, my world and everything I lived for changed immediately. I always loved music and from the moment I woke up until the moment I went to bed I listened to music, sang, wrote, and made noise on a guitar with two strings I once got as a present from an uncle.

But this day changed everything. I discovered true stereo. Not the fake panned-mono recordings they had called "stereo," with all the instruments panned hard left and right. No, this was a sonic panorama, a canvas painted with sound. I have this rare thing in my head that makes me see colors when I hear music. It also works the other way around; I can see a painting and hear music with it. This was like an LSD trip for me at age 11!

Thriller was everywhere: on the radio, on the streets, on TV. You could see large billboards and ads all around town, and the buzz was out there. Everyone was talking Michael Jackson. One thing we were very proud of was that the guitar solo on "Beat It" was played by a Dutch guy: our own Eddie Van Halen, born in the Nijmegen — the Netherlands.

Thriller opened my ears. It changed my thoughts about and perception of music. I already knew that music would always play a great role in my life. My family consists of hard-working people and my dad had a vegetable shop. There was no way in the world I could become a sound engineer or producer; I just had to finish school and go to work. But that didn't keep me from making and recording music. Everywhere I lived, I always had a small homebrew studio. As I said, *Thriller* opened my ears. Whenever I record a song and start mixing, I have the sonic soundscape of *Thriller* right in my mind. I try to let my music breathe and pulse. Depth is what I'm aiming for: trying to get listeners sucked in the music with a 3D perspective of mixing.

It's safe to say that *Thriller* is one of my main influences, although my music doesn't sound like it at all. It's the placements of instruments and the mixing part that have affected the way I work on my own music. Before I got my hands on that classic album, I thought that everything had to have his own place in the mix. Bass and drums center, guitars panned left and right, vocals center. After listening to *Thriller*, I realized that there are no laws when mixing. Every time you mix a song you have to try to paint the image you have in your head on the sonic canvas. You can translate the sounds in your mind to tape, and make the listeners a partner of your own created soundscape.

About five years ago, I was an active member of a forum community when the moderator Craig Anderton announced that Bruce Swedien would be participating. I'm ashamed to admit that at the time, I had no clue who he was. After his introduction, I started reading up on him and discovered he was the man behind all those legendary recordings. If you take away the songs he recorded and mixed, a huge part of our musical history gets deleted and there's little left after that.

I was excited and amazed that someone like him was now on the same forum as I was, and for every question I asked him about sound engineering, he replied in a very logical and structured way to me. It felt like I had entered Valhalla. Here I was, that guy in a city next to Amsterdam in the Netherlands, creating my own music in a small bedroom studio, getting advice from the Godfather of Mixing, Bruce "The Platinum Viking" Swedien. The best thing of it all was that he actually listened to my recordings and gave me advice, lectures, and teachings. It's a kind of *The Prince and the Pauper* story: this man of age on the other side of the world in his huge studio trying to pass over his knowledge to this young guy behind his $200 mixing desk.

My mixes went from so-so to wow in those five years. I suck in and swallow every piece of information Bruce gives me, and whenever we're talking about one of his favorite subjects, "early reflections," I try to put everything he tells me into practice. Luckily, I'm married to the best wife in the world, and she doesn't care a bit when I move stuff around the house to place my microphone where I think it needs to be.

There are about ten people in this world that I care about most: my 85-year-old grandmother, my mum and dad, my sister, my wife Rizzo, and my three-year-old son Skip. Among those ten people is also Bruce Swedien: my friend, my teacher, and the man who made sure that his recording of *Thriller* paved my life's yellow brick road of music to where I am now.

At age 11 I could not imagine that one day the man who recorded the album I was playing in my bedroom would call my house and talk to me about music and all the other wonderful things in life.

Bruce, thank you.

Arjan "Boosh" Boes is, and you might have guessed it already, from the Netherlands.

Arjan "Boosh" Boes with family at home in Holland.

ASHISH MACHANDA

When someone asks me what I think of Michael Jackson's *Thriller*, I always flash back to the first time I listened to that album. Bruce's work with Michael has been more than inspirational for me. It has been an immense source of motivation and ideas for a large part of what I do within music and without. To do such wonderful and consistently progressive work is not an act of chance, but thoughtful actions of intent and careful planning.

The first thing that a lot of Michael's music does is get you on the dance floor. That's just what it did to me when I heard "Billie Jean" upon the release of *Thriller* in India. It was at my cousin's wedding in New Delhi. Dancing was a passion for me! The music was just too infectious. The attention to detail in the making of all those albums is a learning experience. From catchy compositions to timeless arrangements and production values, moving vocal lines to beautifully captured and imagined sonic images; it's almost like a little chemistry-process-fantasy experience.

There was a time when I was going through a restless period; trying to find answers to questions such as what would I be doing for the rest of my life? I knew that I would love to be associated with music and movies in some way or the other. I used to play drums for a few bands at that time and I loved what I did. That's about when I started listening to my music collection all over again. I wanted to understand how great records were made. I had never read or made note of credits until that point. I went through one CD after another, one cassette after another, one LP after another, and made a list of my top ten records. This went on for a few months.

Once I had my top ten list, I started exploring and learning about the people that were involved in making these super records. A name that would come up often was that of a gentleman named Bruce Swedien. Other names that were present were (but of course!) Quincy Jones, Rod Temperton, Jerry Hey, and Andrae Crouch, amongst others. Now I was fascinated. What was it about this person that I would keep coming back to him? These were the albums by Michael Jackson. Credits of engineer, producer, drum sounds, songwriter, etc. were found for Bruce on Michael's records. As I went deeper, I learned that Bruce had also been a part of many other albums I enjoyed listening to.

When I started breaking down the records, it became clear that there was a lot of hard work and love that went into making them. Firstly and foremost, the emotional impact was superb. I think this to be the primal and basic energy of any work, to be able to convey its message successfully—to bring together all the elements for a combined purpose. To make us feel something, to make us feel excited, charged, happy or sad; basically emotions. What is distinctly interesting about Bruce's work is that there were other dimensions present, too, with princely finesse, other than the primal energy, sometimes subtly, and sometimes one would not even realize. Like a master painter, his/her painting will have elements that stand out in the forefront, and also have elements and meanings that one will discover only in time. That's the mark of an excellent craftsman, where all appears as if it were meant to be that way. The spaces were wonderful and used very musically, and when needed, dramatically. What seemed to be employed were basic fundamentals of psychoacoustics and careful blending of direct versus reflected sounds. But the execution is immaculate! That's what the masters of any craft do. And this is noticeable especially in the work where Bruce has also been involved closely at the tracking stage of recording he eventually would mix. The principles and tools that Bruce stands by to this day bring a unique sonic personality, critical in their contribution towards making some of the most memorable and enjoyed records of the electronic era.

Who would think that that this kid from a little city in India would chance upon a multi-Grammy-winning engineer and producer, 6'3", who looks like Santa and sports a handlebar moustache? All I could think of when I met Bruce for the first time at my recording engineering school, Full Sail, was to get answers to several of my questions, which I had saved from many years before. Why was the snare drum level dropped a little just when Michael's voice was introduced in "Billie Jean" from *Thriller*? How was the total blackness (in audio) achieved at a particular point in the track "Keep the Faith"? On *Dangerous,* why was the compressor saturation allowed to be left at a particular spot in "Earth Song"? On *HIStory,* etc. Bruce was kind enough to answer these and many other questions

Ashish Machanda in his studio in India with his daughter.

without any hesitation, proudly! And much to the dismay of some of the people he has worked with, he maintains that there are *no* secrets in this business.

It is unfortunate that a lot of negative publicity has somewhat clouded Michael's reputation and achievements. But I do know and recognize that what Michael Jackson, Quincy Jones, and Bruce Swedien have contributed to this planet is something that no one can take away or ignore! It has to have influenced you in some way or another.

I consider it a privilege to be mentored, respected, and loved by Bruce Swedien.

PETER WADE KEUSCH

It was Hanukah, 1982, when my parents gave Michael Jackson's *Thriller* to my sister and me. Memorizing every song, we listened to it so much that we burned the grooves out of the vinyl. We quickly realized we were onto something big when everyone at school was doing the moonwalk. Years later, after a move through the tunnel to NYC, I was an aspiring record producer working as a runner at Sony Music Studios. I started voraciously reading album credits and discovered Bruce Swedien's name on *Thriller*.

Having recorded at home and in various studios, I had learned all I could from books and needed refining to record professionally. I had an aggressive synthesized sound, filled with computer tricks and sophisticated editing, but my vocals and acoustic instruments were never quite right. Fortunately, Sony was a revolving door of the world's top artists, producers, and engineers, so it was only a matter of time before Bruce Swedien (and his army of equipment racks) arrived.

Bruce came in to record the orchestra for Herbie Hancock's Gershwin album, but despite my efforts, I was unable to get on the session. As luck would have it, he picked up another mix and I was assigned as second assistant. Bruce's mix used a number of simple, solid techniques, which I immediately took home. I saw instant improvement in my own music. He made the studio space his own, turning the lights low, listening carefully, and visualizing the mix, and then charted the song on paper to create a dynamic map. The channels were purposefully left unlabeled so that he would force himself to mix intuitively. His work was elegant, and it resonated profoundly.

A few years later, we met again. I had worked my way up and was engineering top hip-hop, R&B, and pop records for Sony. I'd begun recording Jennifer Lopez' album *This Is Me... Then* when she decided she wanted a special sound. The magic word "Thriller" came up. I was finally going to get to work with Mr. Swedien!

This is where I really got to know Bruce, working alongside him, observing and absorbing his methods and insights in a collaboration that extended to three albums with Jennifer Lopez. Over the years, the techniques he employed for vocals, acoustic instruments, reverbs, and compression all traced back to the recurring theme that less is more. (As a secondary education, I also witnessed his mastery of navigating record label politics, and the correlation between a creative studio atmosphere and happy artists translating to great recordings.)

Back in '81, as Bruce tells it, Quincy Jones challenged him to develop a new sound—something previously unheard—to give *Thriller* its own unique sonic footprint. He spent days developing new techniques, experimenting with new equipment, and employing tools both in and out of the studio. Neither time nor money figured as a restriction. Bruce's chief mission was simply to innovate.

We didn't have that sort of freedom on *This Is Me... Then*, but Bruce insisted on excellence and innovation every step of the way. I was amazed at how he had embraced non-linear hard disk recording (my specialty at the time); not surprising when you consider that this is the same man who had embraced *stereo* when it was new technology. (Sorry to date you, Bruce!) He has been a driving, prolific, and innovative part of every movement of recording, from the days of mono, to multitracking on analog tape, to digital tape, to computers, and he is constantly inventing new sounds and new techniques as gear and technology advance. *This Is Me... Then* became a shining example of Bruce's rigorous commitment to modernity; it's work that I'm proud of, and continue to reference in my mixes.

Eventually I came to focus more exclusively on producing music and recently wrote and produced five songs on Jennifer Lopez' album *Brave*, a project in which Bruce's support has been both treasured and inspiring. Back in 2006, when Bruce and I were in the U.K. recording the London Symphony Orchestra for Jennifer's "Como Ama Una Mujer," I played him the first of my songs that she had recorded, a very personal and demanding track called "Never Gonna Give Up." I remember telling him that, believe it or not, 25 years of listening to *Thriller* was all over this string-laden love song. His reply was nonchalant: "I guess *Thriller* was a pretty good album," he said. "Now what are we gonna do when we grow up?" The legacy of *Thriller* lies not only in its unrivaled hits, sales records, legendary spawning of dance crazes, music videos, and modern sounds, but also the very marked and definite bar it set for production and engineering excellence. It was Bruce's constant experimentation, focus, and commitment that culminated in the benchmark *Thriller*. His continuing efforts to establish something new have been a driving force of inspiration, support, and hunger for that level of innovation and perfection in my own music.

Bruce ended up mixing "Never Gonna Give Up" in his studio in Ocala, Florida, and—just when I thought I knew what to expect—he blew me away by using only *one* compressor on the entire mix! (It was an LA-2A on Jennifer's lead vocal.) I still have a lot to learn.

2008

A tall guy from Teaneck, Peter Wade is an acclaimed Grammy-winning producer/ composer/artist. He has worked with singers including Jennifer Lopez, Marc Anthony, Lindsay Lohan, and Natasha Bedingfield, and also develops new talent out of his Manhattan studio. After earning a degree in civil engineering at Washington University in St. Louis, Peter embarked on a nationwide tour DJing reggae music with his band the Skalars before he moved back east to engineer records at Sony Music Studios Manhattan. Three years recording and mixing hits for top artists under the tutelage of Cory Rooney, Tony Maserati, and me inspired Peter to form a production company, WonderSound, in order to focus on his own projects (the Yeah, Mr. Sack, Shitake Monkey). In 2004, Peter teamed up with singer-songwriter Michelle Lynn Bell to form Lynn & Wade LLP.

In addition to sculpting the sumptuous voice of worldwide pop, Peter can be found collaborating on films, videos, and art pieces for WaNa, a production collective he co- founded in 2004, where he provides sound design, music, raw unbridled inspiration, and omelettes. Peter is also a dormant graffiti artist (WAE32) whose name decorates rock clubs, DJ bars, and a smattering of gas station bathrooms from NYC to L.A. He's an Aries and loves tomato soup.

Checking out a new microphone—a Royer—at Hit Factory in NYC.

CHAPTER 3

MORE ON BRUCE SWEDIEN

LOOKING BACK 25 YEARS:
THE BRUCE SWEDIEN INTERVIEW:

A QUARTER CENTURY WITH
THE BIGGEST PRODUCERS
by Mr. Bonzai
November 6, 2006

Mr. Bonzai talks 25 years of music-making to Bruce Swedien, including his work as co-producer and engineer on Michael Jackson's classic albums Thriller, Bad, and Dangerous, and his current work with Jennifer Lopez and many more top acts.

Bruce Swedien was born in 1934 and discovered a love of recording through a present from his father at just ten years of age. He eventually made a career out of music and first hit the big time in the 50s and 60s recording Duke Ellington and Frankie Valli and the Four Seasons. He met Michael Jackson out in L.A. while working on the movie *The Wiz* and then went on to help record some of Jackson's biggest hits. He has also worked with Mick Jagger, Diana Ross, Count Basie, B. B. King, Paul McCartney, and many more huge stars. MixBuss' Mr. Bonzai recently caught up with Swedien to discuss the last quarter century of music-making.

So we're looking back at your 25 years of music production.
Tell us what you were doing back in 1981?

I was working on *Thriller*. When you go into a project like that you have no idea how important it is going to be, or how important it will be to the industry. When we decided to do that record, it was Michael's second album after *Off the Wall*. If you remember that period of time in the industry, the focus of the young people's attention was away from pop music, and was moving toward video games and other things.

I will never forget the first day we started *Thriller*. We walked into the control room of Studio A at Westlake on Beverly Boulevard; Quincy (Jones) first, then Michael, then me, and then Rod Temperton. Quincy turned to us and said, "We are here to save the music business." But music doesn't work that way. You can't throw a million dollars down on the table and say, "OK, this new album has to sound a million dollars better than the last one." Art doesn't talk to money. But Quincy gave us the mandate to save the music business, and we made a tremendous impact.

Since those days, how has the technology of your work progressed?

Actually, I love what is happening with technology. When digital audio workstations first came into the picture, they were underdeveloped, or ahead of their time and not exactly what we wanted to use for making a musical statement. But now, I use one every single day. And remember, with analog, you don't just put any old analog tape machine in the signal path and expect to get the sound of *Thriller* out of the loudspeakers.

When did you first embrace the digital revolution?

In a big way, it was when Quincy and I did the George Benson album *Give Me the Night*. We were at Kendun Studios in Burbank, and I mixed that entire project to the Soundstream process. This was 1980 and it was totally new for the time. It's a fantastic album, and it was my first real jump into the digital arena.

I had them bring the recording equipment to Burbank, and then I had to go to Salt Lake City to edit and assemble, because that equipment was so huge. That part of the Soundstream process was not easily moveable. Then I brought it back to Hollywood and Kent Duncan mastered it. It was quite a revelation, that the sound of digital was so different from analog. But if you go back and listen to that album, it sounds pretty good. It got some Grammys and sold a ton of records.

How have things progressed since then for you?

Well, I have totally embraced the digital process, as far as multitrack goes, especially now with the deeper bit rate and higher sampling frequencies. I recently did a project for a Brazilian artist in Rio de Janeiro, and did all of the mixing 24-bit, 96K and I am really happy with the results.

Do you still use any analog tape?

I have my Ampex ATR in the control room at home, but I don't think I've used it for a year. I'm afraid to move it out the door, but if I have a project I really care about, I am perfectly happy to do it 24/96K. But you must understand, I use the Universal Audio 2192 converters, which in my estimation are the supreme front end for the digital audio two-channel workstation.

What about consoles over this past 25 years?

The console that I have in my studio at home is the same model Harrison that I did *Thriller* on, a 32C series. That isn't the console that I would use for everything, but sonically and in many other ways, that console is very satisfying. But here at Midnight Blue in Miami for this Jennifer Lopez album, I am using an 80-input SSL J series, and that is about the best super-analog desk today. It has the greatest combination of sound and tools aboard.

What are your favorite microphones and pre-amps?

Interesting question, because I was recently working with Jennifer Lopez, and I was in London recording the London Symphony Orchestra as part of her project. It's an incredible orchestra, about 50 musicians, and we recorded at Angel Studios in London, a converted church. I called my pals at Neumann and told them I wanted to use three TLM-150s with my Decca Tree, and they immediately took care of it. I was talking with Wolfgang at Neumann, and he asked me if I remembered that it was his and my 50th anniversary. In 1956,

I bought two Neumann U-47s and that was the start of our relationship. One of those two mics was stolen when I was recording *Thriller*, but I still have the other one and I still absolutely adore it.

Do you use any other mics from the past?

I have a couple of AKG C-12s that I like a lot, but there is nothing that quite sounds like that U-47. Actually, there is a young man in Finland, Martin Kantola—I did a master class at the Sibelius Academy in Helsinki about ten years ago, and I met this young man who really knows more about microphones than any one single guy I have ever met. He's building a microphone, and I have one of those. I used that for Jennifer. Inside the mic is a classic U-47, but it sounds so good. Jennifer loved it. He calls it the NU-47, but I don't think it's for sale. Björk has one, I have one, and Martin has the only other one. It's the most unbelievable mic I have ever heard.

OK, so what about monitoring?

I have my Westlakes and they go with me everywhere. Quincy says that moving with me from studio to studio is like moving the Fifty Army. It takes 25 Anvil cases to move my speakers, mics, cables, and stuff. Even with the industry in the condition it is in today, I still get calls to do gigs with all my stuff, and it costs a fortune to move. In those cases are my Westlake speakers and my Electrocompaniet monitor amplifiers. I use an amplifier made in Norway, and I use the Westlakes that Glenn Phoenix designed, and they are passive bi-amps. There is no electronic circuitry in the speaker. The monitor amps are connected directly to the drivers. And I use Monster Cable, which I love.

Do you carry reverbs with you?

Well, there are one or two that have stood the test of time that I have in my personal arsenal, that go with me. One is the EMT-250, and I have a 252, which is also a fantastic unit. Typically, the older EMT units are discrete, but not necessarily Class A. With the 252, I use the 250 software, so it's like having two 250s, but one does sound a little different. I also have a Lexicon 480, and I have several custom programs in that. And I have a Lexicon 224 with me. One of my favorite reverbs is the AMS RMX.

Can you pick a few moments in the past 25 years that were especially memorable?

You know, my wife Bea spends a lot of time with me in the studio, and she also travels with me a lot. After working with Michael over the years, one of the most mind-blowing experiences is working in the studio and then going to see him in concert. Bea and I went with him to Japan, traveled all over with him, and we don't know that Michael that gets up on the stage. We have never met him. It's such an unusual thing. As a performing artist he is incomparable. When he steps onstage he becomes another person.

What recordings do use for reference,
to gauge the environment when you go into a new place?

Well, I have my own speakers. I usually go back to some of the old recordings I did in 1959 and 1960 with Count Basie. And I am also so enthusiastic about a project I just did with the Brazilian lady Eliana Elias, on RCA. I will be taking that record around with me.

Who would you like to work with in the future?

Well, I feel like I have worked with just about everybody I have wanted to. But there is a musician and performer I like a lot: Lenny Kravitz. I have met him, and we've talked and tried to get our schedules together, but it hasn't worked out yet.

What do you think about the Internet and downloading?

Well, I love iTunes, and as long as it is done properly and the music is paid for, I think it is perfectly all right.

What about Surround sound?

Well, I hate Surround. Actually, I should say I hate what has been done in Surround, because I think it is a big, bad reflection on our industry. I am not proud of the way that the way our industry has looked at Surround. It is a way to add huge billing to a project that is already over budget. And most projects have no need to be done in Surround anyway. When Surround catches up with the music, and can be done with the entertainment level in focus—not the gimmick level—then I think we might have something to work with and for. But right now, I think Surround is a whole lot of doo-doo.

As you look back, what stands out in your memory?

Quincy and I discuss this. Where my family comes from in Scandinavia, a major goal is retirement. They all say, "Uncle Bruce, when are you going to retire?" Quincy and I have an answer for that. All our lives we have lived out the goal of retirement: to travel around and do what you want all day. That's all I've ever done. Why should I change? I do the projects that I want to do, at my own pace, as I want to do them. I don't see any need to do anything different.

Do you have a favorite motto?

Well, I do some teaching, like the master class at UCLA, and other colleges. I have a motto and it is short and sweet: "Music First." That's all you need to know.

Any advice for the up and coming producers and engineers?

First of all, be serious, and you have to love what you do for the sake of the music. If your goal is a financial one, you are going to fail horribly. If your goal is to make the best music that you can, to the best of your ability, you are going to succeed heroically. And that's the way it works.

Text and photo © Mr. Bonzai
Mr. Bonzai graduated from the University of California, B.A. English Lit. with minor in Art & Film. After college, he was writer/performer in the improvisational Praxis Theater, and co-founded Strangemouth, a radio comedy group that broadcast live in the U.S. and Canada. As creative director of Canada's top-rated CHOM-FM, he served as announcer, writer, and producer, and upon his return to the U.S., managed Lyon Recording Studios, also operating as in-house producer/announcer/engineer.

Since 1980, Mr. Bonzai has written over 1000 articles for magazines in the U.S., Europe, and Asia, including over 500 interviews with leading musicians, artists, directors, producers, and media figures. He has published three books: Studio Life: The Other Side of the Tracks, Hal Blaine: The Story of the World's Most Recorded Musician, *and* Faces of Music. *In television, he has performed and written for "Club Rhino" (Heritage Ent. and Rhino Records for ABC) and "Rock Commandos," a behind-the-scenes music documentary.*

A monthly columnist for Sound & Recording *(Japan), his photos and articles have appeared in* Rolling Stone, Billboard, Mix, EQ, Pro Sound News, Artist Pro, Keyboard, EQ, Daily Variety, Hollywood Reporter, Los Angeles *magazine,* Disney Channel Magazine, Computer Life, *and the* Los Angeles Times, *as well as leading music magazines in England, France, Germany, Austria, Australia, and elsewhere on the planet.*

BRUCE SWEDIEN, THE MENTOR:
A DUTCHMAN REFLECTS
by Han
June 2004
Somewhere in the north of Europe

On Wednesday August 24, 1960, it is hot and humid in Chicago. Count Basie's band with singer Joe Williams is playing in a club and after that, in the middle of the night, they go to the studio for a recording session. A young guy who calls himself Brucie the Viking is engineering, and imagine the tools he's got; nothing like big boards and 24-track Studers. The mics are awesome, though, and so is this young engineer — one of the pioneers in stereo recording and mic placement. This young lad is kind of stubborn in a positive way and very inventive. He's not satisfied with the way recording is commonly done and finds his way to better placements, better sounds, and better-sounding records, due to his skill and talents.

Forty-six years later, this young guy, who never got old, sends an email to a 63-year old guy in Holland, with an attachment of that recording from 1960 in MP3 format (that is supposed to sound not so good as a format). So I download this attachment and open it in Adobe Audition. The first thing that's exceptional is the picture I see: this is the opposite of what we hate so much in the loudness war. It's dynamics all over the place. Then I hit the button and the next thing that happens is that I fall out of my chair from amazement.

I have never heard such a great sound coming from my small Altec Lansing computer speakers (with a small sub). The trumpets, the upright, piano, saxes and trombones — gorgeous sound and an amazing stereo image. I am flabbergasted. The singer comes in, with only bass, piano, and a little drums and a counter melody played by trombone. That is so freaking great, really amazing. This bone sound is coming from somewhere in the garden of my neighbors. Never heard such a thing.

Remember, this was done 46 years ago by great musicians, but also by a young guy in his mid-twenties, who made a recording that is one of the best sounding ever. There was not such a thing as the internet, where everybody can read everything about microphones and placements and where anyone can find everything he needs for making his recordings better. Bruce found it out the hard way, by stumble and fall.

And what I like the most about Bruce is that he will answer all your questions, no matter how complicated, difficult, or silly they are. Unlike someone like Rudy van Gelder, for example, who will take all his secrets with him in his coffin (what's the use?), Bruce is sharing all of his knowledge and skill all over the internet.

Kudos for Brucie the Viking. We love you, man! (At least I do.)

And now I'll put this recording on an USB stick and I'm gonna listen to it on the big main monitors in the CR.

Thank you so much Bruce. I'm honored, really!

Peace.

For me, there have never been secrets involved in anything that I do. I want everyone in on everything that I've learned. It's all for the music!

BRUCE SWEDIEN, THE ENGINEER: PRESS CLIPPING, 1957

This was published in a Chicago Music Publication in 1957, when I was working at the RCA Recording Studios on Navy Pier:

"One of the unsung heroes of the record business is the recording engineer. He can be an arbitrary, disinterested person that does his job, but in a sense without heart or feeling. On the other hand, he can be the link that welds a session together. Such an engineer is RCA's Bruce Swedien. Aside from being a fine technician, his greatest value, at least to me, is his ability to understand and to deliver the sound you are trying to achieve. Another thing I like is his ability to offer a suggestion without ever actually intruding. And when it comes to editing tapes, he's a master. I'm sure this little discourse won't get him the presidency of RCA, but it will at least let him know how I feel."

JOHN JENNINGS, ROYER LABS

Bruce is a big man with a big heart and one of my favorite people ever. It's an honor to be in his life.

I go back about ten years with Bruce, but his contribution to my life goes much further than that short time would imply, both professionally and in one of my most cherished friendships. I'm part owner of the ribbon microphone company Royer Labs. In our early days, ribbon mics had fallen off most engineers' radar and our goal was to bring ribbons back to mainstream recording. A number of key people helped us, but Bruce's contribution was, and is, immeasurable. Bruce is a long-time fan and user of ribbon mics. When he endorsed Royer in our early days, it seemed like half the engineering world decided that if Royer was good enough for Bruce, Royer was good enough for them too. Later, when we introduced our phantom-powered R-122 ribbon mic, the concept was radical and we had a hard time convincing anyone to give the mic a shot. But when we ran an ad with Bruce saying that the R-122 was his favorite ribbon mic, the response was astonishing; it was like we'd run ads in every pro audio magazine on the planet. We couldn't keep R-122s on the shelf. That speaks volumes about the respect that the recording community has for Bruce and his opinion on anything related to recording.

Bruce loves his gear. One day at his house, I mentioned how good his stereo speakers sounded, and he said "Oh, I mixed *Off the Wall* on those speakers." How many people can say *that*?! Then we talked about the stereo recordings he made of some of the great sessions he recorded in the 50s and early 60s. He still has those original tapes. I asked if he was sure he'd be able to find a good machine to play them back on, and he said, "John, I own the machine I recorded these tapes on! When I play them again, it's going to be on the original machine." That machine, along with loads of great microphones, pres, compressors, and other recording gear, much of it bought new by Bruce decades ago, are still with him and in perfect condition. He always said "Respect your gear," and it shows.

Regarding his approach to mixing, one evening I played Bruce a recording of a trio giving an excellent live performance. He listened to two songs, and then said "They're good and this is a good recording, but I could only listen to it once or twice." I asked him why and he said, "The engineer captured this event perfectly, but to me that's merely taking dictation. I'm not interested in taking dictation—I'm into creating a sonic fantasy." To illustrate, he played me some mixes of a Swedish band he was working with. The mixes were absolutely alive and magical—he had created a signature Bruce Swedien adventure and dreamscape in the stereo field. *Thriller* is one of the epitomes of Bruce's approach—the whole intro is one big fantasy, an amazing piece of music and make-believe. A Bruce Swedien recording is never boring!

In 2000, I heard a working mix of a Michael Jackson song Bruce was recording. It sounded like a complete mix. Bruce explained that when he records, he tries to mix as he goes so as not to lose the magic of the individual moments that make up the recording. He said, "You never get back to your instincts. You've got to mix when your instincts are up. I have Quincy Jones to thank for that." That's *great* advice for any engineer.

To really know Bruce, you have to know his wife Bea, one of the most vivacious, mischievous, and fun women I've ever met. I have pictures of her on my office wall—a friend recently thought she was Lauren Bacall. I'll never forget talking with a slightly morose Bruce during a session at Marvin Gaye's old studio in L.A. while Bea was at their home in Connecticut. I said "You're missing Bea, aren't you?" and he replied in his deep voice, "John, she's my life." He meant it. More than his beloved music, the center of Bruce's life is his love story with Bea. You'll see her in these pages. I've had many drinks with Bruce and Bea—the more we have, the more Bea's wild jokes and stories fill the room, while Bruce laughs and beams at her. He's got his share of wild stories, too! But he's happy to hear Bea tell them, filling a room with her charisma and cracking up everyone in earshot.

The Swedien house is regularly filled with pets and visitors, so dinner at the Swedien house can become a real event. Friends bring their kids (many of whom become extended parts of the family)—you sit down to eat and there's tons of food, good drink, lots of talk, much attention paid to any stories the kids have to tell, and then there's Boo, their huge Great Dane, walking around looking down at everyone's plates. He's so big his head is above tabletop level. What a zoo! And a hoot.

In 2005, we were in Toronto, where Bruce was speaking at the MIAC convention. I went over to have breakfast with Bruce and Bea in their hotel room one morning, and the fellow who brought our food up said to Bruce "You look a lot like a sound engineer I've been studying," and then went on to excitedly tell us about his Bruce's recording career. I'll never forget the look of complete shock on his face when Bruce put out his hand and said, "Thank you for those kind words. My name is Bruce Swedien." The guy was blown away—I'll never forget it. I took a picture of the two of them and the fellow says it's one of his most cherished possessions.

We had dinner in Toronto's CN tower during that trip with our friend Dave Dysart (Royer's Canadian distributor) and word got out that Bruce was there. The cellarer invited us back into the wine cellar and treated us to a nice bottle of champagne with cheese, and of course Bea started cracking jokes and goofing off. The photos we took in there are priceless—a bunch of nuts having a total blast.

When Bruce released his book *Make Mine Music*, there was a buzz about it at that year's AES (Audio Engineering Society) convention. There were so many people carrying copies around that I started taking pics of them holding the books up near their faces: Al Schmitt, Elliot Scheiner, Leslie Ann Jones, Chuck Ainlay,

Eddie Kramer, Rupert Neve, Michael Wagener, Dirk Brauner, Russ Long, Terry Howard, Frank Wells, and Dave Hill. Back at Royer we made a collage of the photos and sent it out to Bruce. You'd think we gave him a Rolls! He was so appreciative, and the college is hanging in his studio, West Viking.

Bruce has made some of the most thrilling and influential recordings of our time and has earned his place in history as one of the great masters of his craft. But I have to say that as a person, he's a gem. Say goodbye to him on the phone and his good friends are likely to hear, "I love you." Get off the phone with Bea and she'll say, "Kisses." And they mean it, every time. Bruce is a big man with a big heart and one of my favorite people ever. It's an honor to be in his life.

John Jennings in front of some of his Royer ribbon microphones.

John Jennings is a man on a mission: "I want to put ribbon microphones in the hands of everyone who records music." John got his start, like so many audio professionals, as a guitar-slinger and singer in rock bands in Philadelphia. A phone call from a friend with a recording deal got the car wheels headed west, landing John in Hollywood. After paying dues as both a player and a singer in studios and on stage, John decided to put on the suit and make some money. He took a detour into the corporate world, becoming VP of sales and marketing for a Los Angeles–based data and telecommunications firm. Eight years later he decided to ditch the suit and combine his sales and marketing experience with his rock and roll soul.

In 1996, an introduction to David Royer led to the founding of a new pro audio company: DVA. While DVA ultimately closed due to production problems, the feeling of being on the right path and the knowledge gained from the experience set the stage for the next venture with David Royer. Two fortuitous things transpired; the first was David's fascination with ribbon microphones and the second was a meeting with Rick Perrotta and Rafael Villafane. Realizing a need for the warmth and musicality of ribbon mics in the more clinical world of digital recording, which was coming on strong, the new partners set out to turn David's designs into a marketable reality. After many discussions and numerous business plans, the new company went into production in 1998 and John got busy handling the sales and marketing. The Royer 121 was unveiled at the 1998 AES show. Eight years of seventy-hour weeks later (John's a workaholic—make this man take a break!), the Royer name is known around the world and has become synonymous with the finest in microphones. John Jennings serves as vice president of sales and marketing for Royer Labs.

An ad, telling all engineers to choose the new Royer 122.

ART NOXON, ACOUSTIC SCIENCES CORPORATION

Art Noxon of Acoustic Sciences Corporation reflects upon the impression Bruce has left on him through the years:

I spent half the night tonight fooling around with a new speaker setup at home. Nothing too special. But I listened to as much as I could stand of about two dozen albums looking for a good ride; something that justifies the new speaker setup, not to mention my listening time. I was so disappointed and kept on searching, album after album, for a clue, some justification for my new setup. And then I found Jennifer's *My Way*. Played it and damn. Was it my system or is it just you doing your magic? I'm not too sure. But I do know that your work is the one and only one that sounds so good. You know it does, but still, I just gotta tell you.

That album is done totally on a level that no one else gets close to. I can hear her words and still feel the music. No one musical component is sacrificed because of the presentation of another. It's a clean home run. I just wanted to tell you, it's like I have searchlights highlighting a skywriter that is penning the sky; a dark sky that is backfilled with the instantaneous sparkle and lingering smoke of exploding sky rockets. Your mic work and mix is so damn clear, so full of sound, and yet so full of separated, non-overlapping detail at the same time. And by that process, so easy and engaging to listen to. Blur-free sonic juggling. Other albums seem to somehow sonically overload, pushing too much sound, too much overlapping bandwidth. I think you try to set up a huge dynamic bandwidth and then separate and nail down the instrumentals and vocals without bandwidth overlap. You do not deliver a blurred information package.

I think I should somehow study your mixes, decipher them, and then write an AES paper on your formula for making sonically clear presentations, where the feeling of the music is delivered along with clear lyrics and sonic sparkle. So many other mixes are overloaded with overlapping bandwidth—I can almost see the EQ pumping, like a comb made out of road flares. Bad mixes have a flat EQ instead of lumped EQ with separate musical bandwidths, one next to the other. I'm positive that this is the basis of the clarity of your mixes. You keep clarity by delivering musical power that does not have overlapping bandwidth. That's my guess and I know there is more to it, but I think I've clearly seen at least part of your formula.

Anyway, thanks for making music that pops—crystal clear and yet full of sound, hence fully engaging. And it's not because I'm her fan, which I completely am (she can do no wrong). It's about the mix. And before the mix, it's about the mics the setups and the tracks. Maestro B! Doctor Tone Nailer. Master Sonic Carpenter. Thank you and good night.

The Attack Wall in my own home studio in Ocala, Florida.

CHAPTER 4

MORE ABOUT THE RECORDING PROCESS

AN AUDIO PRIMER: A SHORT INTRODUCTION TO STUDIO PRACTICES AND THE EQUIPMENT BEING USED

In the next few pages, I'll try to give you a better understanding of the work that goes into recording the music that is the subject for this book, and also introduce you to some of the equipment being used. This is not meant as an audio course, but if builds some curiosity, we sure would encourage anyone to check out the more formal education being offered around the world today. Those that want to know more about the specifics of this work, please visit my website — www.bruceswedien.com — were you can find answers to your questions, or even pose your own questions. For me there is only one thing that really counts, and that is that there are no secrets.

For most, the recording studio is something that is far removed from their everyday experiences, and it might also be considered something with quite an amount of mystique around it. For those that work in a studio as sound engineers, it soon becomes a routine; within that reality, it's difficult to see all the dreams that surround and engulf it. Hopefully we will be able to answer some questions through this section of the book. We will try our best to translate this into something that all readers can relate to.

ROOM LIGHT LEVELS DURING THE RECORDING AND MIXING PROCESS

Among the five senses, people depend on vision and hearing to provide the primary cues for conducting the basic activities of daily life. Every moment of our life, we use at least one of our five senses. Our five senses are sight, hearing, taste, touch, and smell. When it comes to recording and mixing, the first thing that comes to my mind is the fact that the human being is primarily a visual animal. If we can discipline ourselves to listen to and mix music in a very low-light environment, we will tend to react and function more in tune with our very basic instincts, especially the sense of hearing. This is very important.

Personally, I favor a low level of light during the music recording process in the studio and control room. Have you ever heard someone say, "Turn down the lights, turn up the music"? Isn't that a great saying? A proper low light level in the studio and control room during the recording and mixing process is very important. The mood created by low lights in the control room and studio can be musically stimulating. Low lights can help us get more in tune with our instincts when recording and mixing music.

Using your instincts when mixing music can become an incredible tool. It will help you "know" what the music must sound like to be effective and above all, entertaining. Once you learn to trust your instincts, you will somehow "know" what musical values are essential. You may not know exactly how and when things will happen (the actual musical events themselves), but all the characteristics along the way become clearly visible, and the end result is musically far more believable. The ability to trust your instincts takes a long time to master. Even given that knowledge, most recording people can't ever seem to accept their emotions when it comes to recording music.

I constantly refer to my earliest mixes of a song—even more so, to my computerized mixes of the original rhythm track recording session, to get back to my very first instinctive reaction to the music: the moment it first influenced me. That is the only time that I will be genuinely able to react to the music emotionally and not cerebrally. It's only at that point in the recording of a piece of music that I will make sound volume level and color judgments that are totally emotional in their relationship to each other, as perceived by my psyche, with all my musical experiences subconsciously affecting the outcome of what I am doing with the music at that moment.

Me at the Record Plant in L.A. Note lava lamp and fruit lights!

A studio is a home away from home—make it your own space!

I LIKE TO THINK OF MY STEREO SOUNDFIELD AS A "SONIC SCULPTURE"

I always try to make my stereo soundfield far more than merely two-channel mono. In other words, I always try to make my stereo soundfield multi-dimensional, not merely left, center, and right. For me to be satisfied with a soundfield, it must have the proportions of left, center, right, and depth. Since the middle 1960s I think my philosophical approach to using the stereo space has been to take the listener into a new reality that did not, or could not, exist in a real-life acoustical environment. This new reality, of course, existed only in my own imagination.

What I mean is that before what I call "the recording revolution," our efforts were directed towards presenting our recorded music to the listener in what amounted to an essentially unaltered, acoustical event; a little slice of life, musically speaking. (This "recording revolution" took place from 1950 through 1970.) This was not true just of myself, but was also true of many of the people that were interested in the same things that I was. We all experienced this same "recording revolution." After that change in our basic music recording objective, along came the new reality in using the "stereo space."

There is almost nothing else in my life as important to me as recording music. I love to listen to live music, but to me the real central interest of my being is in creating recorded popular music that communicates emotion to the listener. It has been said that for eons, music has articulated the personal to whole groups of people. I believe the reason for that is that music can voice authentic feelings and sentiment. People respond to music that contains the components of real emotion and feeling. It has always been very natural for me to feel strong emotions about the music I am working on.

THE ACUSONIC RECORDING PROCESS

When Quincy Jones, Michael Jackson, and I were recording *Off the Wall*, we wanted to coin a catchphrase to represent my recording technique with multiple multitrack tape machines. So we came up with the phrase "the Acusonic Recording Process." To my continued amazement, I am frequently asked to explain, "What *is* the Acusonic Recording Process?" In fact, on several occasions I have been offered impressive sums of money by recording studios and companies that wanted to purchase the Acusonic Recording Process, thinking that it was a "black box" that recorded sound could be processed through.

I recall one awkward circumstance, several years ago, when I got a phone call in the studio from someone's secretary, saying that a photographer's team from a very respected, very important, foreign trade journal was in an airplane on the way from somewhere overseas, to shoot a cover photo of the Acusonic Recording Process machine! I don't remember exactly what I did, but I do recall mumbling something to the highly confused photographer about the machine being "away for repairs" indefinitely, and we'd have to reschedule the photo shoot!

On my last lecture trip to Japan and Europe, I did admit to the press what the real deal with the Acusonic Recording Process was. This is the basic concept that spawned the catchphrase "the Acusonic Recording Process."

The Acusonic Recording Process is, in reality, merely a name that Quincy and I came up with to describe my recording technique with more than one

Thriller has probably collected more awards than any single album in the history of music—and it has also become the best-selling album in the world.

A note from
Michael during
mixing.

please Bruce
when ever you do a mix
have the key board
at this level

THANX M.J.

Michael on stage
with Jennifer Batten
on guitar during
the *Bad* tour.

M J J PRODUCTIONS
COMMUNICATIONS DIVISION

Bob Jones
Vice President
Communications &
Media Relations

June 25, 1990

Mr. & Mrs. Bruce Swedien
4950 Moorpark Rd.
Moorpark, CA 93021

Dear Bruce & Bea:

Your kind sentiments expressed during my illness were so
thoughtful and very comforting.

With your prayers and blessings as my shield, I am quickly
advancing towards complete recovery. I fully expect to
resume work in the near future and continue sharing the
fruits of my labor with loyal friends such as you.

Thank you for standing by me. You're wonderful!

Love always,

Michael Jackson

10960 Wilshire Boulevard   Suite 2204
Los Angeles, California 90024   (213) 478-7966   FAX (213) 478-7614

A letter from Michael.

Pictured while working away on the song "State of Shock" on the Jacksons' *Victory* album. From left: Me, Bea, Mick Jagger, and Michael.

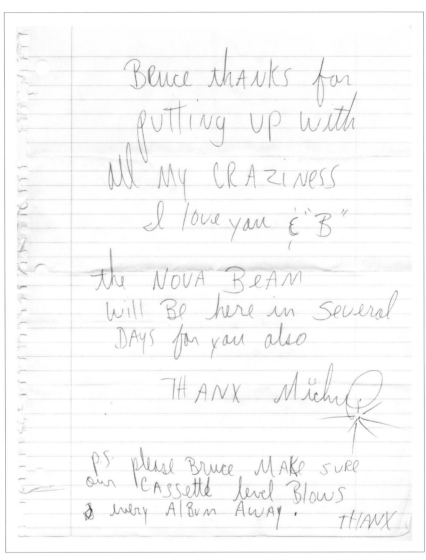

One handwritten note from Michael during a project.

A tape box from Westlake Studios with a drawing made by Michael during one of the long sessions while making *Thriller*.

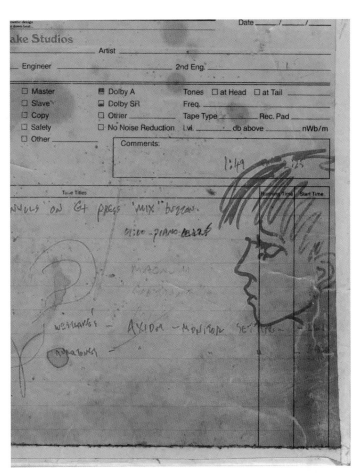

The subway scene in *The Wiz*.

Quincy Jones conducting the all-star choir for "We Are the World."

Me, Vincent Price, and Michael Jackson during the recording of Vincent Price's rap on "Thriller."

A note from Michael on "They Don't Care About Us" during the recording of *HIStory*.

In the studio, Michael with members of the Seawind Horns and me.

Michael as the Scarecrow in *The Wiz*.

While in the studio, Michael steadily did a lot of drawings. Here are some studies of a few characters in one of the studios.

With *Off the Wall*, we really started collecting awards! And who Clara and Clarence are, we leave to the reader to find out.

multitrack recording machine. The phrase is essentially a combination of the words "accurate" and "sonic." I figured the "accurate" part of it referred to the accuracy of true stereophonic sound imagery. The "sonic" part of it referred to the fact that it is sound that we are trying to characterize.

TAPE MACHINES AND MULTITRACKING

In the 1970s, the number of tracks that I used to record Michael's music really began to increase. Multitrack music recording began with four-track tape machines (on which the Beatle's recorded much of their music). And then it moved on to eight-track, 16-track, 24-track, and even more.

In 1981, I used my 16-track, two-inch analog tape machine without noise reduction, to record drums and percussion on some of the songs that I recorded with Michael. By using my 16-track, the additional track width on the tape, when compared to 24-track, gives much less self-generated tape noise, thereby eliminating the need for noise reduction. In addition, the sonic quality of 16-track as a music-recording medium is, to my ear, the most convincing.

The top panel and deck controls of "Big Legs, Tight Skirts!"—the 16-track machine used for many tracks of Michael Jackson's music. Straight into the machine without any noise reduction at all—the result is hard to beat!

Photo by Phil Cochlin.

"Big Legs, Tight Skirts!" is the name that Quincy coined for the 16-track, two-inch tape machine responsible for the incredible drum and percussion sound on many of Michael Jackson's recordings. Straight into the machine without any noise reduction at all—the result is impossible to beat! Using 16-track analog, as compared to 24-track analog, also gives improved transient response. And by not having to use any noise reduction, there is much less unwelcome coloration of the sound quality.

I began recording Michael Jackson's music with analog multitrack tape machines. Then I went to digital multitrack tape machines, and lastly digital audio workstations. In actuality, I think that multitrack recording itself has probably been the most important tool of all in recording the music of Michael Jackson.

By the late 1970s, 24-track recording machines were pretty much standard equipment in the larger music recording studios. Recently, however, in the major studios, most of those tape machines have been replaced by digital audio workstations.

The one man who championed the call for more recording tracks in the studio is Les Paul, who, through his cooperation with Ampex, developed the very first eight-track recording machine. It was, of course, an analog machine.

Les Paul performing circa 1990 at Fat Tuesdays in New York City.

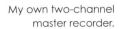

My own two-channel
master recorder.

Working with Michael gave me the opportunity to make use of all the wonderful new tools that the industry offered at that time. It was also a great learning experience for me. Michael and Quincy generously gave me enough time to make good use of these incredible new music-recording devices. It was a great time in our lives in the recording studio.

By linking several multitrack machines together, I was able to utilize the great number of tracks that were needed to realize Michael's songs in the manner that we thought necessary. I think that having so many tracks available to me gave me the opportunity to record many more true stereo images in the sound fields of Michael's music, by using pairs of tracks in stereo.

This one fact more than any other probably has made my work sound different from anyone else's. I did find out soon that when a song begins to approach 100 tracks or more, there would be a lot to organize. No problem! In actuality, I love it!

At one point in the recording of Michael's music, I linked three 24-track, two-inch tape machines together with SMPTE (Society of Motion Picture and Television Engineers) time-code. This system gave me a total of 66 tracks of audio to record on. There was one track on each machine dedicated to syncing SMPTE timecode and one track on each machine dedicated as a blank guard track between the SMPTE, which made a nasty cross-talk noise if it leaked onto the audio tracks.

I am a life member of SMPTE (pronounced SIMP-tee), a professional organization that writes the standards for records, film, and video recording systems used in North America. When they wrote the specifications for SMPTE timecode, they made it possible for all manufacturers to use the same techniques for reading and writing timecodes so that everybody's tape and equipment would work together.

Today quite a few engineers and studios still like to use an analog recorder for their initial tracks, later converting them over to digital for editing and mixing. It is especially when it comes to editing that digital really lends itself very well to the creative process. Digital makes everything readily available and it makes all forms of editing, and much more, far easier and indeed a lot quicker than one was used to during the analog day. Counting tracks is hardly an issue these days; it is all available for anyone from even the cheapest solutions on to the more costly studio installations that might include computer solutions that look more like what you could find only in big corporations just a few years ago. We're on the verge of something that might see some dramatic changes in the years to come—music will survive but the distribution will certainly change.

The author with three 24-track Studer machines.

A CASE FULL OF MONSTER CABLE GOES WITH ME EVERYWHERE

Over the years I've learned that, in music recording, it's the supposedly insignificant details that are often overlooked that can, in actuality, turn out to be extremely important. In fact, Quincy Jones and I discuss this very subject. Q has said to me, "It's *all* important!" I think I am lucky in that I absolutely love details in anything that I am involved in, especially music recording. I'm such a nutcase that I even carry my own wire to every project that I do!

In 1987 when Michael Jackson, Quincy Jones, and I were beginning work on Michael's *Bad* album in Westlake Audio's beautiful Studio D, my pal Noel Lee (of Monster Cable fame) called me and said that he had something new that I absolutely had to listen to. The very next day Noel brought a big box and a heavy-duty wooden spool of heavy-duty gray audio cable to me at the studio.

I was working on a mix. It was pretty near finished. I thought to myself, "I would love to hear Noel's new cable on the mix, in the signal path between the desk output and the input to the stereo master recorder." That was the first time I had a chance to compare really superb cable to ordinary wire. As Noel predicted, I heard a definite improvement in sound quality! Michael and Quincy came in the control room and I asked them to listen to the mix with the new Monster Cable in place. They were knocked out by the incredibly improved detail in the sound. Since then my heavy-duty case full of Monster Cable goes with me everywhere. My beautiful little studio at home is entirely wired with Monster Cable.

Not long ago, Noel Lee called me again, and said that he had another new product for me to try. He said, "Bruce, you'll love it!" Noel and I frequently talk about audio technique and recorded sound in general. We don't always agree on all the audio issues, but we do wholeheartedly agree that all those issues are important. The next week he sent me a Monster Model MP Pro 7000. It is a rack-mountable power center with clean power and 12 outlets. Noel said that I should connect all my reverbs, microphone pre-amps, CD players, and outboard gear to it. I did. Wow! Big improvement in sound quality and a much lower noise content in each of the devices that I powered with it. I bought it right then and there.

MICROPHONES ARE THE HOLY GRAIL

Am I satisfied? I really don't think so. I guess I am still looking for the Holy Grail of music recording. What could that be? It would probably have to be the most superb microphone available, as far as I am concerned. My microphone collection now numbers more than 105 fantastic mics! As you no doubt can see, I absolutely love microphones.

However, I am still looking for that "ideal" microphone. I have always had a never- ending quest for the best!

My search for that Holy Grail in music recording began when my father and I purchased an old movie theater on Nicollet Avenue in Minneapolis in 1954. We built my first real studio in that great place. It is still a world-class music-recording studio today.

One of my first big investments in music recording equipment was in 1953 in Minneapolis when I bought my first two Neumann/Telefunken U-47s. (I only have one of those gorgeous mics left; the other one was stolen during the *Thriller* sessions in Hollywood.) When I bought my Neumann/Telefunken U-47 microphones, they cost $390.00 each. At the present time, I have turned down an offer of more than 30 times that amount for this incredible microphone!

There are basically three types of microphones in use in most music recording studios today. They are: dynamic microphones, condenser microphones, and ribbon microphones.

Let's start with the dynamic microphone, how it is constructed, and how it works. Dynamic microphones are versatile and ideal for general-purpose use. They use a simple design with few moving parts. They are relatively sturdy and resilient to rough handling. They are also better suited to handling high volume levels, such as from certain musical instruments or amplifiers. They have no internal amplifier and do not require batteries or external power.

As you may recall from your school science, when a magnet is moved near a coil of wire, an electrical current is generated in the wire. Using this electromagnet principle, the dynamic microphone uses a wire coil and magnet to create the audio signal. The diaphragm is attached to the coil. When the diaphragm vibrates in response to incoming sound waves, the coil moves backwards and forwards past the magnet. This creates a current in the coil, which is channeled from the microphone along wires. A common configuration is shown below.

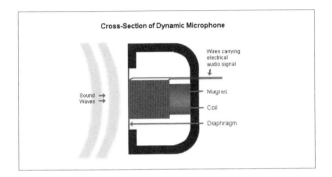

Dynamics do not usually have the same flat frequency response as condensers. Instead, they tend to have tailored frequency responses for particular applications. Neodymium magnets are more powerful than conventional magnets, meaning that neodymium microphones can be made smaller, with more linear frequency response and higher output level.

Then there is the condenser microphone. Condenser means capacitor, an electronic component that stores energy in the form of an electrostatic field. The term "condenser" is actually obsolete but has stuck as the name for this type of microphone, which uses a capacitor to convert acoustical energy into electrical energy. A capacitor has two plates with a voltage between them. In the condenser mic, one of these plates is made of very light material and acts as the diaphragm. The diaphragm vibrates when struck by sound waves, changing the distance between the two plates and therefore changing the capacitance. Specifically, when the plates are closer together, capacitance increases and a charge current occurs. When the plates are further apart, capacitance decreases and a discharge current

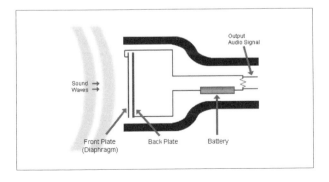

occurs. A voltage is required across the capacitor for this to work. This voltage is supplied either by a battery in the mic or by external phantom power.

The electret condenser mic uses a special type of capacitor, which has a permanent voltage built in during manufacture. This is somewhat like a permanent magnet, in that it doesn't require any external power for operation. However, good electret condenser mics usually include a pre-amplifier, which does still require power. Other than this difference, you can think of an electret condenser microphone as being the same as a normal condenser.

Condenser microphones have a flatter frequency response than dynamics. A condenser mic works in much the same way as an electrostatic tweeter (although obviously in reverse).

My Neumann U-47.

The ribbon microphone is the last type we're going to introduce. The air movement associated with the sound moves the metallic ribbon in the magnetic field, generating an imaging voltage between the ends of the ribbon that is proportional to the velocity of the ribbon—this is characterized as a "velocity" microphone. In most cases, due mostly to the physics of its construction, a ribbon microphone comes with a figure of eight pattern characteristic, something which lends it very well to "Blumlein" techniques when recording. That is when two microphones meet in a 90 degree angle and has been explained in more detail in another part of this book. Here, the point is to give an idea of how various microphones work and what use they might be put to.

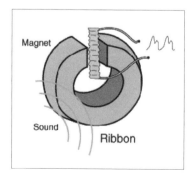

Advantages:

Adds "warmth" to the tone by accenting lows when close-miked.

Can be used to discriminate against distant low frequency noise in its most common gradient form.

Disadvantages:

Accenting lows sometimes produces "boomy" bass.

Very susceptible to wind noise. Not suitable for outside use unless very well shielded.

USING MICROPHONES

Shure SM-7 dynamic microphone.

One of my absolutely favorite microphones is the Shure SM-7. It is a super high quality music-recording microphone. I have used this superb mike to record many of Michael's lead vocals. In fact, I recoreded most of the big hit records of Michael's career with him in front of one of my SM-7s.

The first one that I bought, I bought new in 1977 from Westlake Audio in Hollywood. It is one of the first SM-7s to be used on a major music project. It's serial number is 252. It sounds absolutely fantastic! I still use it on every project that I do. I used it several times on James Ingram with equally stunning sonic results!

Ribbon microphones are something totally different when it comes to recording. All ribbons, like the RCA models 44 and 77, are extremely fragile due to the physical limits of the microphone — they even need to be stored in an

A Neumann M-49, the first ever remotely controlled condenser microphone.

upright position in order not to damage them. More modern ribbons, especially those from Royer, are much more robust and can be stored horizontally with no problems at all. Ribbons will react to impulses in a very different fashion compared to condenser microphones, and in direct comparison they might seem to sound a little dark. For recording acoustic guitars and percussion, ribbons can indeed lend a very important quality to any recording,.

THE DECCA-TREE MICROPHONE SYSTEM
IN THE YEAR 2001, WORKING WITH MICHAEL JACKSON

The album was Michael Jackson's album *Invincible*. We were working at Hit Factory/Criteria studios in Miami, Florida. The song was a piece of music, called "Whatever Happens," that Michael had done in collaboration with Carlos Santana; a beautiful piece with a large orchestra and a beautiful string arrangement by Jeremy Lubbock.

We were already working on Michael's project at Hit Factory/Criteria, so we decided to record the orchestra at that studio as well. I was a bit doubtful at first about recording a gorgeous orchestra arrangement in Miami. We would usually record the orchestra on a major project in New York, Los Angeles, or London. The arranger, Jeremy Lubbock, had recorded a large orchestra in Miami before. He told me that the string players in Miami are absolutely wonderful. He was right!

Hit Factory/Criteria is an absolutely fantastic new facility, definitely: cutting edge and state-of-the-art as far as major recording studios go. (Actually, Criteria Studios in Miami was bought by the Hit Factory Studios in New York just a few years ago. It has undergone complete redesign and renewal.) However, the studio does not have a Decca Tree microphone system. I just had to have a Decca Tree for this session! What should I do?

I called my old pal Wes Dooley, at Audio Engineering Associates in Burbank California, and asked him if he could send me one of his fabulous new Decca Tree microphone stands to use for this very important session. A couple of days later it was delivered to me at Hit Factory/Criteria in Miami. Neumann Microphone Company was kind enough to send me three brand new M150 omni-directional microphones to use on the Decca Tree for this session. The M150 was so new that at the time that I did these sessions, that there were only two of them in all of the United States! Neumann sent me those two mics, and then the morning of the session, with the orchestra, the third M150 arrived from Berlin!

To clearly understand microphone technique, we need to start with a brief discussion of how sound is generated by musical instruments. I think things became much clearer to me when I realized how important it is to conceptualize my own idea of what the stereo space in music recording actually is: the space that our soundfield occupies between the speakers. First, I try to think of the stereo space as a piece of musical reality. Once we have acquired that concept, we can conversely also think of the stereo space as a piece of musical fantasy. Whether or not it could exist in nature, or in a natural acoustical environment, is irrelevant. Most of the stereo spaces in my recordings began their lives in my imagination. In reality, the space that my thoughts and efforts genuinely inhabit is the *gap between the speakers.*

Wes Dooley of Audio Engineering Associates, AEA, with one of his ribbon microphones.

RECORDING VOCALS

"The Way You Make Me Feel" is a good example of Michael Jackson's incredible vocal talent. Michael sang all the parts on this song. Nothing in this remarkable recording is sampled or copied in any way. We had no pitch correction or any such device at this point in time in the studio: we relied entirely on Michael's own incredible sense of pitch. The sense of space in this recording comes from how I used the microphones by moving Michael back a few paces for each subsequent take. That creates a feeling of space by keeping the early reflections in the recording space intact.

I have always felt that in order to trigger an emotional response in the soul of the listener, music, to me, must be close to the primitive. "The Way You Make Me Feel" is also a good example of this. At first, the word "primitive" bugged me a bit. I thought perhaps "primal" might be a better choice. I was wrong, "primitive" is the best choice. After thinking about it for a bit, "primitive" suggests aboriginal origins to me, and that is exactly what it is about certain pieces of music that pushes my button. As my thesaurus says, it also suggests "the cobwebs of antiquity." I got the idea from Duke Ellington in his description of music, and why it appeals to him. He did use the word "primitive."

Keeping the music close to the "primitive" has always been a very important issue for me. I think that this is one reason for the sound of my work. Basically, I think that I have always sought out, or tuned in on, the primitive or earthy rudiments in the music that I am involved in. Then I will try to focus my attention on those elements in my presentation of the sonic canvas of the music. This can, most definitely, be true in classical music as well as popular music. For instance, Ravel's "Bolero" is quite primitive in concept, to me (e.g., its repetitive and very "earthy" rhythms).

I think Igor Stravinsky had the same idea when he said: "My music is best understood by children and animals." What did he really mean when he said that? Samuel Johnson called music "the only sensual pleasure without vice." Very interesting. John Phillip Sousa, of all people, wrote, "Jazz music will endure just as long as people hear it through their feet, instead of their brains." Popular music may be America's classical music. Future generations may remember only pop, jazz, and country as the true American music.

I've always felt that if a lesser artist than Michael Jackson had sung "The Way You Make Me Feel," it would never have seen the light of day! I used my Shure SM-7 on Michael's lead vocal. Recording vocals for any type of music requires a good deal of thought and preparation. Whether it be a single solo voice, or a choir of eighty voices, or a back-up chorus of five singers, there are many things to consider. First, the type of music to be recorded is most important. Pop, jazz, rhythm and blues, country or classical—they each require a different approach. The biggest single difference in studio mic technique for vocal recording for me would be in the recording of vocal sound sources in classical music, contrasted with the recording of pop vocal sound sources. The first and most important consideration is that I would never mic the vocalist in a classical recording as closely as I would in a vocalist in pop music recording.

Second, the vocal effect is important to consider. In other words, in a group vocal, is a choral effect desired, with a large massive sound, or should it be a smaller, warm intimate vocal group sound? Occasionally, a mixture of the two can be musically very pleasing.

Good choral recorded sound is best achieved, I think by using as few microphones as possible. The singers should be placed well back from the microphones. This vocal recording technique places most of the sound mixing responsibility on the room acoustics and the vocalists. Obviously, this recording approach requires an excellent studio or a room with extremely good acoustics.

This technique coupled with really good singers and a fine room will give a result that is not merely satisfying but a thrilling musical experience. A close-miked vocal group sound requires several mics and places most of the sound mixing responsibilities on the engineer. It also removes a great deal of acoustical support from the sound. When using this technique, it would probably be best to first divide the miking by voice quality, and next by harmony parts in the vocal arrangement. As a rule of thumb, you can figure four or five singers will require two mics, and ten singers five mics. The singers work from six inches or less to two feet or more from the mics. With excellent singers, the result is very pleasing. When doubling, or stacking, vocal parts, I like to do a layer with the singers moved back from the mics enough to add some early reflections to the sound.

In choosing a microphone and recording technique for a solo or lead vocal in a pop or rock vocal recording, the most important thing to consider is the vocal timbre of the artist. To review, timbre is the sound characteristic of the voice—i.e., is it soft and breathy, or is it loud and penetrating? Your choice of vocal microphone should be made on the basis of the vocal quality of the artist and the sonic personality you want to project, and nothing else. In this instance, we must remember to think of music recording as an artist would think of trying to capture a scene on his canvas. (Our canvas is our recording medium.) Like the artist, we cannot capture the true reality of the scene, and it would be a fallacy to even try. We must project our interpretation of that reality. As in everything else in music recording, there are no set rules so at first, you must realize, some experimentation is usually in order.

What may seem to be an obvious choice may not work well at all. After a bit of experience you will be able to hear someone speak, or rehearse a vocal part, and instinctively know what mic will be a good choice. Extreme equalization is most definitely not the way to achieve a superb vocal recording, though a small amount of EQ may be beneficial. If you find yourself having to apply a great deal of EQ to the mic channel to achieve an acceptable vocal sound, it's time to try another microphone. Here are some suggestions:

Well-rounded, naturally good-sounding voice:
Neumann U-47 tube mic
Telefunken 251
AKG C-12

Sony C800-G
AKG 414 EB
Neumann U-87
Neumann U-67

Thin, weak voice (using the proximity effect to dramatize the low register):
RCA 44BX

Loud, brassy voice with good projection:
Shure SM-7
AKG 414 EB
RCA 44BX

Good voice but too sibilant:
Shure SM-7 (wind screen)
RCA 44BX
Neumann U-87 (wind screen)
Neumann U-67 (wind screen)

Of course, this list could go on and on but these suggestions should give you an idea or two.

Stacking or doubling a lead vocal is helpful. Frequently, during the doubling process, I will change the tape speed of the master recorder slightly during the recording of the double (or pitch down the cue mix coming from the digital audio workstation), and play that to the vocalists while recording the double. During this process, the amount of pitch change used should be very small. To use this vocal recording technique you must have a singer that is extremely good, with an excellent sense of relative pitch, because, of course, changing the speed of the tape machine when recording the double changes the pitch of the basic track. When this sped-up or slowed-down vocal double is combined with the original, it seems to add a bit of sonority (a full, rich quality) to the lead vocal that makes it more interesting. I ordinarily slow the music playback down during the recording process, not speed it up, if I am using this technique.

If I am working with a digital audio workstation (DAW), the process is almost the same. I will pitch down the cue mix coming from the DAW and play that to the vocalists while recording the double. The amount of pitching down that I do is usually only three or four cents in pitch. When mixing a double of a lead vocal track, I will frequently keep the double at a slightly lower level in the mix than the basic lead vocal track. This serves to add support to the vocal without making it appear to be an obvious trick.

The final playback medium of the recording is important to consider when preparing for a vocal recording. Whether the eventual product is to be monaural or stereo should influence your vocal miking technique. If the eventual hearing medium is going to monophonic, and if it is a complex vocal arrangement with few singers and a lot of harmony and interacting parts, you will probably need more mics than if it is a basically unison background vocal arrangement. By adjusting mic levels during the recording process, we can make sure that each part in the arrangement can be heard clearly and in its proper relationship to the other parts of the vocal arrangement. This, of course, is true to a degree in stereophonic recording, but monophonic recording gives no "panoramic" acoustical support to the vocal parts. If the final product is a stereophonic recording medium, I always try to preserve as much natural, acoustical stereo sound as possible and then keep this audio information as close to the original soundfield as possible right through to the final mix.

Here is an explanation of how I would record a vocal group of five singers. My first mic choice would be two high-quality, good condition, large-capsule condenser microphones such as the AKG 414 EB, or my matched pair of Neumann M149s. These two beautiful classic microphones are sequential serial numbers. They are superb and perfect for high quality vocal recording. The singers are positioned facing each other. The mics are placed close together, back to back, about four inches apart or less. This method of keeping the mics close together allows some mixing of sound to occur acoustically. It also gives good phase coherency so that when the mix is heard monaurally there will be no change in balance or quality. (Phase coherency is achieved by keeping the mics close together so that the sound sources arrive at the two mics at about the same point in time, thus minimizing phase distortion.)

I will record a basic vocal track using two channels of the multitrack tape, one mic on each track. I would then ask the singers to step back from the mics about two feet or so and record a double of the original part. This also would be recorded in discrete stereo on two channels of the multitrack. It is very important to carefully watch the volume levels of the individual vocal tracks. Keep the levels on the individual vocal tracks as consistent as possible. By having the singers step back from the mics during this vocal pass, in order to keep the track levels consistent, we are forced to raise the volume level of the two mics on this pass, thus giving greater acoustical support to the sound.

Finally, I will normally mix these four tracks in the final mix in the same proportion on the same side of the stereo panorama as they occurred during the performance. In some recordings I hear of vocal groups, I hear the stereo tracks flopped over or reversed in the stereo panorama in the final mix in an effort to get a mixture, or as my old pal Phil Spector calls it, a "Wall of Sound." The problem with this, to my ear, is that the acoustics also mix in reverse order. This, technique, to my way of thinking, removes much of the personality, or character, of the recording environment from the soundfield, sometimes resulting in a bland, not-too-interesting vocal group sound.

I must take this opportunity to point out that this matter is entirely a matter of personal taste.

Very often, in vocal recording, I hear a lot of single, monaural tracks merely panned either left or right in a half-hearted attempt at stereo sound. All this really creates is left and right mono and has nothing to do with the support of music. "Two-channel monaural" has absolutely nothing to do with stereo recording, and affords little or no acoustical support to the recording. The additional effort and planning required to preserve real stereo and the acoustical support it provides is well worth it.

I always start by trying to think of how a record that I am doing will sound ten years from now. By keeping the musical sense of a piece of music uppermost in our minds, the music that we record today will sound just as good years from now as it does to us today. Will a microphone choice, a microphone technique, a reverb or sound processing device of today make the music sound hopelessly dated in the future? Think of it like this: it would be like doing a recording years ago and using one too many wah-wah pedals on the guitar parts. Don't put one too many processors on the music just because the effects are in the control room.

When recording vocal duets, I will look for microphones for the vocalists that have an obviously different sonic character. This difference in microphone character will add to the already different timber of the two voices and make the resulting sonic picture more fascinating.

The Shure SM-7 that I used with Michael Jackson for his vocals.

Another microphone that I have, and that I bought new in 1954, is my Neumann U-47—seen here in its original box. This microphone has been used on artists ranging from Joe Williams with the Count Basie Orchestra, Sarah Vaughan, and James Ingram on to Michael Jackson and Jennifer Lopez. This is a microphone that really shows how mature microphone technology was at that time already.

RECORDING AND MIXING DRUMS, VOCALS, AND OTHER SOUND SOURCES

My favorite reverb for drums is my AMS—RMX. I will normally use the ambience program with about a 125 ms predelay to allow the early reflections in the original recording to be heard. In the mix process, I generally use a high-pass setting of about 100 Hz for all drum sources except the kick. This allows the kick drum to occupy all the space below 100 Hz.

I am often asked whether, for recording and mixing lead vocals, I prefer close miking or miking from a distance. Generally speaking, I love close miking for lead vocals. The technique of close miking eliminates almost all but the direct sound of the vocal (or the instruments). If I were recording and mixing a slow ballad (a tempo of about 75 BPM) I would usually use my EMT 250 or 252 on the lead vocal, set for about 1.8 sec. reverb time with a predelay of 100 to 125 ms.

I never EQ the mix buss.

I've had to respond to the following question often — it shows that at least there are a few people that are truly interested is high-quality music recording: "100ms predelay on drums sounds surprising. When I use a long predelay on drums I usually get a noticeable and undesirable 'slapback' effect. There must be a generous amount of early reflection in that to smooth that over, or is the reverb attack somehow muted?"

My matched
pair of
Neumann
U-149s.

An M-149
close up —
you can see
the selector
for pick-up
patterns:
omni through
cardioid to
figure-of-eight.

100 ms is close to the *shortest* reverb predelay that I would use! More often than not, my predelay amount would be in the order of 125 to 132 ms! Try that setting for predelay on vocal or orchestral parts as well. The reverb attack is *never* muted!

Here's what happens (I'll start by saying that you need a pretty nice acoustical space to record in). Early reflections are something that I have always considered "the forgotten factor" of acoustical support, when it comes to high quality music recording. (Except in my recordings! I always give early reflections a great deal of thought and consideration.) The thing that is always apparent to my ear is that the quality of early reflections when generated in a room is quite different (and vastly superior) to the so-called "early reflections" that would be generated artificially (if you can)!

So, if we have well-recorded sound sources, with good early reflections, what you want to do is to open up the predelay, or make the predelay larger in number, to accommodate the early reflections. If you have done a good job of recording your sound source, if you don't have predelay in the reverb you'll mask these beautiful early reflections. And those early reflections are a very important component of sound, very important.

Our ability as music listeners to localize the direction and to form some judgment of the distance that we are from a sound source, under ordinary conditions of listening, is really a matter of common experience. When we listen directly to an orchestra, we form a sense of spatial relation to the instruments of the orchestra. And to me this has always meant that this spatial character of the sound gives to the music a sense of depth and expansiveness. It's what I would call an attempt to preserve the music in true auditory perspective, so this makes it necessary for us to record some sort of stereophonic reproduction; not merely virtual left/right intensity differences, but a sense of space.

I've always felt that music is three-dimensional. Recorded music, in order to be interesting and different-sounding to the ear from ordinary music recordings, must have three dimensions, not just two dimensions. The dimensions are of course, left and right, but the third dimension is depth. This is the most difficult to achieve in modern recording, so it is imperative that it be there. If it isn't, the sound tends to be very monochrome, dull,≠ and uninteresting. Unfortunately, most of recorded sound today falls into that category, but it is possible to achieve depth and width at the same time.

LARGE-SCALE MIXERS

For those of you that do get intrigued by what these mixers can do, we will try to explain in a way that would make it all a little more appreciated—and this book even more enjoyable to read. By today's standards, one would hardly call the Harrison 3232 mixer extensive, but at the time when *Thriller* was recorded it was, and for the production of the music and all other audio that went on that album it was essential indeed!

Mixing can in parts be compared to making food. It really doesn't matter how good the quality of the individual ingredients are—if they are not put together in the right manner it will never please the eater. Different cooks make very different meals out of the very same ingredients, and the same can be said for sound engineers—no two will give you the same result. But one thing they will give you is their own sonic personality. On the next page you will be presented with how the Harrison 3232 mixer is constructed and its various functions. Hope it's helpful!

The photo above shows a Harrison 4032 mixer, as was used during the recording of *Thriller*. For those that are not used to a mixer like this it will probably look a little too complicated. In reality it is not—the idea behind the design is pretty straightforward. We will try to give you, the reader, an idea how such a desk works in real life in the studio. A mixer comes with various sections that take care of the different processes that need to be covered during recording and mixing, and it provides the necessary flexibility to make all the tasks at hand as easy to perform as possible.

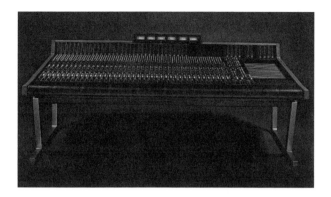

The Harrison 4032 is, as the model number indicates, a mixer with 40 inputs. These inputs are where one typically would connect any source one would like to record or mix during a project. During the recording process, these sources might come from either a microphone or a line-level signal directly from an instrument, or any audio source for that matter (like pre-recorded effects or real-life sounds). When we say 40 inputs, what you then see are 40 identical strips from the left side of the mixer to the right. In each strip, the level will be set first through an input gain control that usually resides on top of the strip. This, in combination with the fader at the bottom, sets the overall level for the recorded signal. The strip also includes an EQ section as well as all routing to the busses of the mixer.

THE BUS SECTION

The photo below shows the buss section on a Harrison 4032 mixer. The model number indicates how many busses the 4032 can supply: where 40 is the number of inputs, 32 is the number of busses—routable buss matrix, that is. This makes for a very flexible mixer, and one that was perfect for the work performed while recording Michael on the *Thriller* album.

THE INPUT MODULE

The photo below shows a Harrison 4032 mixer input module, and in a Harrison 4032 there are 40 of these modules laid across the mixer from left to right. All these modules connect to the busses that make up the mixer and then out to the main stereo outputs in the end. The input modules are in a sense the heart of the mixer, where all the incoming signals are being treated. Looking at the photo, you can see how the module is built up from the input amplifiers at the right through the EQ section down to the fader.

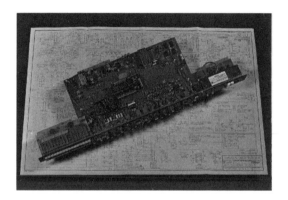

SPEAKERS, AMPLIFIERS, AND VOLUME LEVELS IN THE CONTROL ROOM

Over the years I have been very fussy about the volume levels that I use in the control room. I have always tried to observe the American OSHA sound exposure standards. I like to test my mixes at a variety of volume levels, and on a variety of different speaker systems. This will make sure that the mix will sound good anywhere. If a mix sounds good at a low SPL (sound pressure level), it will sound great at higher levels. Save your ears—we only get two!

For both recording and mixing, I currently use Westlake Audio's Lc3W-12 speaker systems. Glenn Phoenix of Westlake Audio called me one day and said that he had just finished a new speaker design. He suggested that I give it a serious listen. I was a bit skeptical at first about trying any new music-mixing speaker, but I should have known better than to underestimate Glenn when it comes to an audio-design issue.

Glenn brought a pair of his new speakers to the studio so I could check them out. When I sat down at the console to listen, I was absolutely amazed! I have never heard speakers with more points of sound-source definition in the left-to-right panorama. In addition, the low end is spectacular! The scale of the soundfield is flawless.

To me, the mixing phase of my music projects is very personal and can get a bit intense. Mixing is the last phase of a project where I can make an artistic contribution to the sonics of the music, so the speakers that I use are extremely critical to the success of the project.

Of course, any discussion of hyper-fidelity loudspeakers would be incomplete without an in-depth look at the amplifiers that drive those loudspeakers, and the wire or cable that connects the amplifiers to the speakers, and the wire or cable that connects those amplifiers to their source. In most cases, that source would be the monitor output of an extremely high-quality mixing desk.

MONITOR SPEAKER SETTINGS

Here are the standard monitoring settings that I use for all my sessions. To set these values I normally use my Simpson (Type 2) SPL Meter, or a Radio Shack Sound Level meter (catalogue #33-2050).

I. Mid-field monitoring: Westlake Audio Lc3W-12s (placed on top of meter over-bridge of mixing desk)

To adjust the Westlake speakers for an SPL level of approximately 93 SPL (Sound Pressure Level):

A. Set SPL meter
   1. A" scale(OSHA)
   2. Speed: "slow" (OSHA)
   3. Range: 90.

B. Play wide-range complex program material
   1. Set playback for +3 buss peaks on VU scale
   2. Observe SPL results (+3 buss peaks = 93 SPL peaks)

C. Make mark on the monitor level control

NOTE: This will result in a good loud level for mixing popular music. It can be used for a total listening time of four hours of mixing per day. When I mix at this level for two and a half hours and then take a 30-minute break, I don't experience any ear fatigue when using my Westlake Lc3W-12s.

NOTE: If lower record buss levels are to be used, adjust SPL resultant peaks accordingly; e. g., if absolute 0 VU buss peaks are to be recorded, then add 3 db of monitor level before marking the monitor level control.

II. Near-field monitoring: Auratones (placed on top of meter over-bridge on mixing desk)

To adjust the Auratone speakers for an SPL level of approximately 83 SPL:

A. Set SPL meter
 1. "A" scale (OSHA)
 2. Speed: "slow" (OSHA)
 3. Range: 80

B. Play wide-range complex program material
 1. Set playback for +3 buss peaks on VU scale
 2. Observe SPL results (+3 buss peaks=83 SPL peaks)

C. Make mark on monitor level control.

NOTE: This will result in a good Auratone level for mixing popular music. It can be used for a total listening time of eight hours of mixing per day. If lower record buss levels are to be used, adjust SPL resultant peaks accordingly; e. g.: if absolute 0 VU buss peaks are to be recorded, then add 3 db of monitor level when marking the monitor level control.

Do not monitor at extremely high speaker levels. You should be able to carry on a conversation in the control room while you are mixing. If you have to shout to be heard, turn down the speaker level. You will only get one set of eardrums in your lifetime; treat them like the precious things that they are. Who knows, they might be worth a million dollars some day. Go easy on your ears. Permanent hearing loss can occur very quickly in a control room, especially with some of the new, super high-powered monitor systems in use in modern studios today.

Glenn Phoenix of Westlake Audio.

Here we are in my own Westviking Studio in Ocala, Florida: me on the left and Trond "the Norwegian Sherpa" on the right. The speakers in the back are being powered by Norwegian power amps—Electrocompaniet.

OUTBOARD EQUIPMENT

The term "outboard equipment" refers to equipment that is not built into the recording studio in a permanent manner.

THE THRILLER RACK

The first stack from left is, top to bottom:
Eventide 1745 Delay
Two Technics M-85 cassette decks
Eventide 1745 Delay
Lexicon Model 97 Super Prime Time

Second stack, top to bottom:
GML 8200
UREI 565 Little Dipper
Eventide 910 Harmonizer
Innovonics Compressor
Two Dolby 361
UREI 964 Digital Metronome
Orban 526A De-Esser
Eventide H-949 Harmonizer

Third stack, top to bottom:
Lexocon 480L LARC
Publison Fullmost relief-enlarger
High frequency enhancer with de-essing
UREI 545 Parametric EQ
Three UREI 1176
UREI LA-2A

Fourth stack, top to bottom:
UREI 545 Parametric EQ
Two DBX 160
Two UREI LA-4A
Two DBX 160X

The first question to ask ourselves when considering using a specific piece of outboard equipment is "Will it make the music better?" Or are we just grabbing a device, hoping it will be our salvation? In other words, are we hoping it gives us that "magic sound"?

What I have found is that a really good Michael song, or in fact any good piece of music, seems to have a life of it's own.

Here's what I mean: let the song tell us what to do next. If the song doesn't want a "gated reverb" on the snare drum, don't try to force it. If the gated reverb on the snare sounds like doo-doo, try something else. You cannot win out over the musical personality of the song. Try to think of outboard processing devices as machines that by themselves cannot make the music better. We're the only ones that can do that—by making good choices.

I have been very fortunate working on Michael's music in that his music is not only wonderful but it also affords me the inspiration to do my very best and make the best choices.

When I started recording music in the recording studio, electronically controlled reverb, or echo, was not in use. If we wanted signal processing such as echo on a recording, it had to be generated acoustically, and of course, it had to happen during the performance of the music being recorded.

When echo chambers finally were being used in the recording studio, they were for many years analog only, whether they were a room or a steel plate reverb generating device. There were even a few reverb generators in the 1960s that used steel springs as a reverb-generating medium. The problem was that those units sounded just like springs.

In 1980, digital signal processing was in its relative infancy. At that time it cost $10,000 to buy a 16-bit reverb with a high-frequency response of 10,000 hertz, and there were only a couple of companies in the business of manufacturing reverb devices.

Digital delay lines, or DDLs, appeared about the same time as the digital reverb devices. Before the introduction of DDLs, we used a tape machine and would route the echo send signal through it and then to the reverb device, whether it was a room or a plate. As the echo send signal was being recorded and played back by the echo delay tape machine, or "slap" machine as it was sometimes called, the reverb signal would be delayed by an amount of time roughly equal to about 125 milliseconds. This amount of reverb delay depended on the tape speed of the delay machine and the head spacing between the record and playback heads. At this time I used a variable speed control on the reverb delay machine to match the delay time with the tempo of the music.

Reverberation is all around us. It is a part of our everyday lives. To obtain more mixing control. I tend to use close mike techniques when recording Michael. The most important fact to keep in mind is that the *sense* of music must be foremost in what we do. Trust your ears! Listen to your inner voice—your instincts. That little person that rides around on your shoulder and whispers things in your ear is usually right!

I think that to flawlessly reproduce a sound, all frequencies in the audible spectrum must be reproduced with the same intensity. This means that all the components in the signal path, from the microphone to the loudspeaker, must have a flat frequency response.

The role of the equalizer is to control the gain, or volume, of one or more parts of the audio spectrum while leaving the other parts relatively unchanged. An equalizer is in actuality a frequency selective volume control. To me equalization is purely a matter of personal taste. The tone controls on your home stereo are a good example of using a control to change the tonal balance of music to suit our personal taste. (Or lack of same!)

To me, there are really only two groups or categories of equalization to use in music recording: corrective equalization and creative equalization. Both can be overused and can be either helpful or detrimental to the emotional impact of the music involved. The trick is to use as little EQ as possible to achieve the desired result. Extensive use of EQ to correct a poorly conceived and recorded sound invariably sounds artificial.

Heavy EQ and/or Filtering is used to create effects, such as a telephone-like voice quality. That is a valid reason for using a lot of EQ. That is a distinct example of creative EQ.

The real aim of equalization is to either overcome variances in the tonal quality of the sound sources, or to "hype" the sound to achieve an emotional effect in the music. The real trick with EQ, to me, is to use it *gracefully*, to enhance the music and make the sonic image more entertaining.

DYNAMICS

So what do these various units do? Their names say a lot. A compressor compresses the sound, the limiter limits the sound, and the de-esser removes sound like that produced when using words with an S or a similar sound. But there is a little more, and we'll try to explain some of it here.

COMPRESSOR

Before the introduction of the automatic gain control, or compressor, the only way the music dynamics could be controlled was by "riding" the gain, or volume control. Fortunately for us, the introduction of the compressor occured not long after the introduction of electronic recording.

Most compressors are threshold sensitive, which means that signals below a certain volume level are not affected by the device. The user sets this threshold level. Signals above this threshold level are reduced in gain. This gain reduction level is also set by the user and is expressed as a ratio. Compression ratio is expressed in DBs. It means that a certain change in input level will result in a certain change in output level. Response time is pretty obvious, and I think you probably already know enough of the basics about compressors and limiters to get you through a session.

There has from time to time been a trend to use compression on the mix buss of a mix, but to my ear this use of the device will cause a dulling effect of the sonic image. This use of the device will also allow transient peaks to cause attenuation of the whole signal including low-level high-frequency sounds. If the sound sources on your multi-track are properly recorded in the first place they will not need much limiting or compression.

Experiment with all the new signal processors. There is no such thing as wasted time spent messing around with new effects. The main thing is to learn what will work to enhance the sonic image of the music you are involved with.

Developing your own musical ideas is what creating a unique "Sonic Personality" is all about. Don't let the technology control you. Try to remember that just because all these new "toys" are there, it doesn't mean you have to use them. If they make sense in the music and add to the musical sense of the music that you are working on then they belong there.

One last thing about peripheral processors or outboard equipment: I always try to think of how a record that I am recording will sound ten years from now. Will a processing device of today make it sound hopelessly dated in the future? I realize that that is hard to judge, and we have no audio crystal ball to consult on such matters.

Think of it like this: it would be like doing a recording ten years ago and using one too many wah-wah pedals on the guitar parts. So, don't put one too many processors on the music just because the effects are in the control room. By keeping the musical sense of a piece of music uppermost in our minds, the music that we record today will sound just as good years from now as it does to us today.

AUDIO LIMITER

This is a device that prevents an audio signal from exceeding a set level. Contrary to a compressor, which reduces the overall dynamic range of the music, a limiter only affects the highest peaks. You will often see these functions within one unit, a compressor/limiter, where the limiter usually acts at very short attack times (from 1 microsecond to 1 millisecond) and with a compression ratio to its function of something like 10:1. You'll often find a limiter controlling the recording level of a reporter's handheld recorder to avoid accidents from happing and maybe preventing a historic event from being captured.

DE-ESSER

This unit detects and reduces the signal that might be generated while singing or speaking S-like words, something that varies a lot from one person to another. When it comes to singers, you might prefer to go for a pop filter in front of the microphone in order to dampen the motion of air that might occur. A de-esser is more often used for broadcast applications and spoken word.

NOISE GATE

This works like a gate in many ways—it only lets in what you allow it to let in. You set the threshold of where the sound level is allowed to run through. It is often used in situations where you would like to record a source that might come with a lot of unwanted noise, like an overdriven guitar amp, but were you want to keep the performance. It doesn't remove any noise, it just doesn't let it through when there is no playing going on.

EQUALIZERS

This is something most of you probably have a relationship with in some form or another, because in its simplest form you'll find it as treble and bass controls on your stereo, or within your MP3 player, for that matter. Equalizers comes in two basic forms: either with fixed frequency points, usually called a graphic equalizer, or as a parametric, were you can fine-tune all the settings to your liking—not only the frequency, but also the steepness of the curve as well as the boost and cut of the chosen frequency. If you ask me, you'll find out that I don't use equalizers much at all, with very few exceptions.

DELAYS

In this category you'll find units that add various time-based effects to the signal: echo, reverb, doubling, chorus, and flanging. The amount of added delay can be anything from less than a millisecond to minutes, depending on the memory capacity of the delay unit—with today's prices on memory that can easily mean a lot, even with audio of the highest quality when it comes to bit rate and sampling frequency. In the effects rack pictured above you'll see many such units, where some might serve a more specialized function than others, but in essence they all share a few common qualities. This is even more important in the digital audio realm, since there are so many factors that might come to play if you don't take these factors into consideration. What you want to avoid is anything that doesn't speak the same language when it comes to sampling frequency and bit rate; if they don't, you might get some really nasty results. More than anything, these units lend themselves extremely well to the more creatively inclined among us, and ever since Les Paul started to really make all these things possible, they have been used to a great extent in most popular recordings of our time—and today this can be done for almost no money at all compared to earlier times.

Plenty of time-based effects units in this outboard rack.

One of my personal favorites when it comes to microphone preamps. This one, the 610-2, is being manufactured by Universal Audio (UA). It is based on the original, which I started using while working for Bill Putnam at Universal Studios in Chicago in the late fifties. UA is today being run by Bill Putnam's two sons.

MY FAVORITE REVERBS FOR MY WORK
WITH MICHAEL: A LITTLE REVERB HISTORY

When I started making records, electronically controlled reverb, or echo, was not in use. If we wanted signal processing on a recording, it had to be generated acoustically, and, of course, it had to happen during the performance of the music being recorded.

My mentor in music recording, Milton T. "Bill" Putnam, is the man whose many accomplishments eventually became standard, common practice in the music recording industry. For instance, the way we use reverb or echo in modern recording desks is, in essence, a Bill Putnam brainchild. The location and application of the echo send and return controls were first conceived in his fertile imagination. That system has remained almost unchanged from Bill's first rather small recording consoles, to the incredibly powerful mixing desks of today.

Bill Putnam was truly an innovator. He was one of a kind. A bona fide original. I think Bill Putnam had a unique perspective on music recording. He is someone about whom you can rightfully say that he was the first. If you have ever listened to pop music or tried your hand at recording music, Milton T. "Bill" Putnam has touched your life! It was he who conceived the idea of artificial reverberation for artistic effect.

The mid-twenties was really the beginning of electric recording, and recorded reverb was essentially the audible byproduct of a physical distance between a sound source and a microphone. Record companies sought out appropriate rooms for a desired effect. Right from the outset of early recording, those early pioneers were already working with mic placement and rooms for a desired effect! But around the early to mid-thirties, the jukebox was introduced—a great invention, but the thirties were not yet a time for stellar playback systems, let alone recording equipment, and the early jukebox suffered from the early technology. But hey, they had to start somewhere! At the time, reverb from room ambience was practically banned from studios due to how it affected the performance of the jukeboxes. This is the primary reason most recordings from the mid-thirties until the fifties are by design "dry."

As recording and playback equipment improved, so did the opportunities to experiment with new recording techniques, as well as new marketing ploys for playback resellers. Enter the "hi-fi" revolution of the post-war era-- It is commonly accepted that the use of reverb, whether natural room, chamber, or plate, practically defined the "hi-fi" era of music. In the 1950s, an engineer named Bill Fine brought back the popularity of natural reverb as an effect by putting a single mic in a large hall to capture the ambience of a recording. The recording was released on Mercury's *Living Presence* record.

Echo chambers were for many years analog only, whether they were rooms or steel-plate reverb generating devices.

A BEAUTIFUL NYMPH NAMED ECHO
APPEARS IN GREEK MYTHOLOGY

In much the same way as a beautiful nymph named Echo appeared in Greek mythology, reverberation, or echo, appeared in the modern recording studio. With a lovely musical voice, Echo was employed by Zeus to distract Hera with incessant babbling, gibbering, and gossip while he embarked on sexual adventures with his many paramours unhindered. Hera, driven half insane by Echo's inane jabbering, lost patience, took the power of speech away from Echo, and removed her from Olympus. All Echo could do after this was to repeat the last words that anyone had said to her. (Hmm, sound familiar?) After falling in love and being spurned by Narcissus, Echo rejected the advances of Pan, who was willing to overlook her affliction, and who in a fit of pique, smashed her into tiny pieces and scattered her all over the world. That means that if you believe in Greek mythology, she can now be heard by anyone who raises their voice in a reverberant space!

Reverb is essentially echo where the reflections are so close together that the results are perceived as a single continuous sound. Reverberations, simulated or otherwise, are an integral part in the recording process, in live performance, and also in our very perception of our surroundings. In a mix or a live performance, reverb will be used to make a vocal or instrumental performance sound more polished and to fit nicely into the mix, giving an impression of depth and space. Delays and echoes can be used to give more life to parts or tracks in a mix, or to create a dramatic stereo image. Used in conjunction with panning, delays can be used to help create artificial Doppler effects, one of my favorite techniques for adding a bit of theatrics to a mix. Used cleverly in a mix, delay can be subtle enough that it is not obvious when swallowed by the rest of the instruments and can be used to just change the feel of a track by giving it life and space; or it can simply be used to give a dramatic edge to an instrumental part.

Reverb and echo are often associated with religious or spiritual connotations. Churches have been built since the middle ages with dramatic acoustic properties in mind. Religious choirs and orchestras tend to perform in large echoic chambers with reflective surfaces. Can you imagine how dull and lifeless Gregorian chants would sound without all that absolutely stunning reverb? Echo appears to have been employed for religious reasons even before the construction of the dramatic medieval cathedrals. In the twentieth century, with the dramatic rise of recorded music in popular culture, reverberation has been simulated using tiled rooms, springs, plates with transducers attached to them, and now in the modern era, digital computer reverb devices.

ELECTRONIC REVERB SETTINGS

The main settings on a digital reverb or reverb plug-in are predelay, size, reverb time, color, damping, and a setting for wet/dry mix.

PREDELAY

The predelay determines how far the sound source is from the walls of the room. This has the subjective effect of creating depth, and long predelays of 50 to 65 milliseconds are often used to wash vocals and make them fit better in a mix. Sound travels at 1,000 feet per second through air, so a 50 millisecond predelay gives the effect of placing a sound source 50 feet away from the opposite wall of a room. This sounds pretty huge, but it is not unusual for concerts to take place in large concert halls or auditoriums that are considerably larger than 50 feet in length.

ROOM SIZE

Quite simply and as you would expect, room size determines the size of the room that is being simulated. To create a huge spatial effect on a mix element, select a large room size. To keep things tight and close, select a smaller room size. We're treading on some pretty biased territory here. Large room sizes can be used to create exquisite effects on vocals, strings, and on various mix elements. Small room sizes can be used to create very interesting effects on certain mix elements.

DAMPING

Damping can be used to simulate coverings on walls and objects in a room that absorb or diffuse sound. For example, it stands to reason that the smoothly tiled walls at our local swimming pool will reflect sound more efficiently than a wallpapered stud partition that you would find in a newly built house.

COLOR

It also stands to reason that not all surfaces or objects will necessarily reflect sound equally at all frequencies. The color control on the reverb unit or plug-in can adjust the frequency spectrum of the reflections being simulated. Alternatively, the output of the reverb unit could be patched through an equalizer before being returned through the mixing desk. Using lower frequency values for color will generate a "warmer" feeling reverb, while using higher frequency values will generate a "brighter" feel.

WET AND DRY MIX

In addition, it stands to reason that when standing in any acoustic space, one will hear sound waves directly from the source as well as reflections from the ambient surroundings. The levels of these can be adjusted in an electronic reverb by changing the wet and dry mix. In an anechoic chamber, one will hear the dry source almost exclusively as there are close to zero reflections, whereas in a large wood-paneled hall, one would hear a lot of reflected sound.

REVERB TIME

The reverb time of a room is a measure of the length of time, usually in milliseconds, from when the initial sound reflections are set up to when they are attenuated by 60 decibels. This is simulated in a digital reverb and can be anywhere between close to zero and infinity. In a real room, we do not have this amount of control.

PLATE REVERB

In the days before the era of the electronic reverb, plate reverbs were used to simulate spatial sounds in music. Listening to music recorded in the seventies, it is obvious that a lot of the engineers who tuned these devices were immensely skilled in using them.

TIMING A DELAY

It's always been very important to me to have a space of un-reverberated sound in the music before the onset of reverb. This space is most effective when it is tempo-related to the beat of the music.

There were even a few reverb generators in the 1960s that used steel springs as a reverb-generating medium. To me, they sounded just like springs.

In 1980, digital signal processing was in its relative infancy. At that time, it cost $10,000 to buy a 16-bit reverb with a high-frequency response of 15,000 hertz. There were only a couple of manufacturers in the business of reverb devices. Digital delay lines, or DDLs, appeared about the same time as the digital reverb devices. Before the introduction of DDLs, we used a tape machine and would route the echo send signal through it and then to the reverb device, whether it was a room or a plate. As the echo send signal was being recorded and played back by the echo delay tape machine (or "slap" machine, as it was sometimes called), the reverb signal would be delayed by an amount of time roughly equal to about

125 milliseconds. This amount of reverb delay depended on the tape speed of the delay machine and the head spacing between the record and playback heads. Also at this time I used a variable speed control on the reverb delay machine to match the delay time with the tempo of the music. That analog delay sound is very smooth has a character that DDLs have never been able to generate.

(I am going to be setting up that same analog delay system of reverb delay again, because I miss that quality in my reverb sound. I used my Ampex 351 tape machine because the record-to-playback head spacing of 1 1/4 inches gave an almost ideal amount of reverb delay time.)

At this same time, devices such as pitch shifters and digital filters were beginning to show up on the market and soon found use in making music more interesting. They were very expensive by today's standards. In this age of ever-increasing inflation isn't it wonderful that those devices that cost $10,000 can now be had for under $1,000? Technology marches on!

Reverberation is all around us. It is a part of our everyday lives. To obtain more mixing control, we tend to use close mic techniques and remove a great deal of the room feel in much of what we record. I do feel that by now you should have a good idea now of how much the sound of natural room acoustics can enhance any sound image.

To be truly creative recording people, we must also be able to use the new and incredible tools that are now available to make the music that we record more entertaining and at the same time leave the impression of our own individual sonic personality on the music.

As many of you probably know, I still use analog recording a great deal in my work. (At least as of this writing.) I also use digital multitrack machines a great deal. Once the sound of analog is in the music, most of it stays there. I do use digital multitrack technology and all the incredible power it has to offer. The only important fact to keep in focus is that the sense of music must be foremost in what we do. Trust your ears! Listen to your inner voice! Your instincts are usually right!

Most often, I see peripheral processors being brought into the project at the last stage of production, the mix. I like to experiment with processing devices at all stages of the production of a piece of music. I want to know what the effect of this device will be long before I get to that sensitive point in a project, the mix. For me, the mix is the most emotional and trying time during a project. It is the last time that we can do anything imaginative about the music that we are working on. After the mix, the music truly doesn't need us anymore. I frequently find myself in a period of depression after the mix is done. I am no longer a part of what is being created. The music has cut me loose.

As you know by now, I don't consider the mastering phase of my projects as a point in the project to "save" it, or to "fix" anything. If I have trouble with something in the mastering room, I am back in the studio re-mixing to satisfy my problem.

It's incredible to see the fantastic processing devices available now that have so many good effects in one unit! Not long ago when you wanted an effect, you went out and bought a single effect processor. Now those single-effect devices are like dinosaurs. You can now get one unit that has large, medium, and small room reverb effects, gated reverb, reverse reverb, chorusing, flanging, and delays up to several seconds. Most of these processors have a variable reverb delay built in as well.

THE EMT 250 ELECTRONIC REVERBERATOR UNIT

Early in 1976, EMT teamed up with the American electronics company Dynatron to create the EMT 250 Electronic Reverberator Unit. With that, the first "practical" digital reverb was born: the EMT 250—the R2D2-looking, three-foot high digital reverb that would define all digital reverbs in the future. It is a floor-standing unit, and looked like equipment from a seventies sci-fi movie set. The EMT 250 reverb has features that are very impressive. It has not only predelay controls, but also high and low frequency decay times. However, the 250 was more than merely a reverb; it was the really first multi-effects unit. It had modulation effects like chorus and phase, as well as echo and delay. The controls were simple: large lollipop-shaped levers and a few pushbuttons.

There were only 250 EMT 250s made. In a couple of years, the EMT 250 was updated to the 251, which was a similar design with an LCD display and a larger feature set. The 251 offered extended frequency response, additional parameter controls, and more programs. And, in my opinion the EMT 251 didn't sound nearly as good as the EMT 250!

BERNIE GRUNDMAN MASTERING STUDIOS IN HOLLYWOOD AND TOKYO

All of the Michael Jackson albums that I've discussed in this book were mastered by my good friend Bernie Grundman. The reason for that is not just because Bernie has become a good friend. It goes far deeper than that. It is because I think that Bernie Grundman is the very best that this industry has to offer when it comes to mastering popular music.

Bernie is one of the first mastering engineers to cater directly to an artist's needs. He developed and uses one of the first A-B mastering systems in the world.

What this means is that Bernie can use two sets of EQ, level, and limiting controls. While one set of EQs and levels are playing for the cutting of one song, the other side can be set up with alternate settings. This allows incredibly fine control of the mastering process.

I think that the huge success of *Thriller* convinced many record companies that letting the artists have more control over what happens to their product wasn't such a bad idea. Also in the case of the mastering of Michael's records, I always took Michael with me to Bernie's studio when I mastered his albums to make sure that he knew exactly what Bernie and I were doing.

Bernie Grundman and his facility have been synonymous with quality mastering for more than 30 years. I first heard his wonderful mastering work when I listened to some vinyl LPs that he had mastered when he worked for the jazz label Contemporary Records. As I listened to those great-sounding records, I thought to myself, "Wow — that is beautiful mastering! I'd better get to know that guy!"

Bernie Grundman began his mastering career with the jazz label Contemporary Records after arriving in Los Angeles from Phoenix in the 1960s. He later joined the staff at A&M. Before long, he was made head of the A&M Records mastering department in Los Angeles. I first met Bernie Grundman when I was working with Quincy Jones at A&M Studios in Hollywood in 1976, on Quincy's production of Leslie Gore's album *Love Me By Name*. Quincy and I recorded much of the album *Love Me By Name* in Studio A at A&M Studios in Hollywood. Studio A was right across the hall from Bernie's mastering studio.

While Quincy and I were working on the *Love Me By Name,* I went into Bernie's mastering room and introduced myself. He and I hit it off immediately. Bernie is quietly authoritative about his work. That and the fact that he has never found ordinary, off-the-shelf technology solutions satisfactory endeared him to me immediately. I am that way myself. In the following years we did several Brothers Johnson albums: *Look Out For Number One, Blam*, and *Light Up the Night*. We also did some Quincy Jones albums together for A&M Records: *Sounds and Stuff Like That*, *Roots*, and *The Dude*.

Bernie is best known for his mastering work and his own studio, Bernie Grundman Mastering, which he opened in February 1984 in Hollywood. Bea and I had become good friends with Bernie and his lovely wife Claire. Just before Bernie left his staff job at A&M, he called me one day and said that he and Claire wanted to take us to lunch and that they had something very important to talk to us about. We couldn't imagine what! Actually Bernie appeared to be just a bit secretive about the subject. We went to a great little Hollywood restaurant named

Butterfields. It was July 29th, 1983. Not much was said at first. Obviously Bernie had a lot on his mind. Finally Bernie said: "I am going to leave A&M and open my own studio! After lunch we want to take you and Bea to see it!"

Holy cow! You could have heard a pin drop! Bea and I looked at each other and thought, "Jeez, Bernie, should have done that years ago!" I said, "Bernie, that's fantastic!" Claire said, "He's terrified. He's a bit insecure you know—you and Bea are the first to know." I said, "Bernie, you can cut perfect masters with a g--d--- nail! You have nothing to worry about. Do it!"

He did it! The rest is history. Bernie covers all the major formats with the same degree of quality and attention to detail. "The trick is to give the client the highest degree of quality but to do so with a minimum of processing and a minimum of artistic coloration," says Grundman. "We accomplish that with a combination of clean electronics and an open mind." Now Bernie has also established a beautiful mastering studio in Tokyo, Japan with engineer Yasuji Maeda.

Bernie Grundman at work
in his mastering suite.
Photo by David Goggin.

INFLUENCES

There are seven people in my life that have had a profound effect on what I have accomplished musically. I will mention them here in the order in which they came into my life. They are my parents, Ellsworth and Louise Swedien; Bea Anderson-Swedien, who changed my life dramatically!; Milton T. "Bill" Putnam; Edward Kennedy "Duke" Ellington; Quincy Jones; and Michael Jackson.

ELLSWORTH AND LOUISE SWEDIEN

My parents, Ellsworth and Louise Swedien, lived and loved music. They were both accomplished keyboard artists. My dad played the pipe organ and directed our church choir. I think their enthusiasm for the music and work that they were involved in made a permanent impression on me.

BEA ANDERSON-SWEDIEN

I met Beatrice Anderson one summer evening, in a park in Minneapolis, Minnesota. I was 17 years old, she was 16. When she smiled her incredible smile at me, it was over! I can remember it like it was yesterday. I knew instantly that here was the girl I wanted to spend the rest of my life with! Of course the fact that she has that wonderful, fresh-scrubbed, Swedish beauty has put me in awe of her permanently.

When I first started work at RCA Victor Recording, and then a bit later at Universal Recording Studios in Chicago, all the musicians and engineers that were my studio colleagues told me that I shouldn't ever bring my wife to the studio. They told me that if I did that I would be very sorry. At the time, I couldn't imagine what they were talking about. I still don't. I am, of course, a bit contrary by nature, so I immediately invited Bea to visit me in the studio. One of the first times Bea came to hang out with me in the studio was when I was doing an album with Count Basie and Joe Williams at Universal Studios. We were working all night. The sessions started at 2:00 a.m. and ended at 6:00 a.m. Of course, Bea hit it off famously with everyone in the band, and before I knew it, Joe Williams had her copying lyrics for him. She had a great time! So did I! We'll never forget those happy sessions!

When there is a major event in my life, I don't feel that it has actually happened until I tell Bea about it, or until she has participated in the occasion. I have made it a habit to include her in all that I am involved in. I don't go anywhere without her. I am a terrible traveler. In addition, I am not my favorite companion. If I have Bea with me, I am always happy and seem to have a very good time.

Bea is liked by everyone. The people that I work with in the studio would much rather talk to her than to me. (Hmmm.) When Michael Jackson or Quincy Jones calls to talk to me about a project, they are on the phone with me for three or four minutes, then they ask to speak to "Beasie" and they talk to her for half an hour or more! For some reason MJ always wants to know what she is cooking for us for dinner that day. Bea's joy for life is infectious. She inspires everyone around her—starting with me!

Bea has never once complained to me or anyone else about the long hours we spend in the studio. Never a whimper. Of course I do think that because I included her once in awhile, she has seen that in my work, the hours can be a bit long, and the sessions are extremely involved.

Over the years of listening to music together, I have found that Bea has an exceptionally good ear! Plus, she has a fairly average person's perspective, and very good judgment, as well. I love to get her observations on what I am involved in, musically. When I am working on a project — mixing, for instance — I always play my recordings and mixes for her first, before anyone else has heard them. It can be 2:00 or 3:00 in the morning. I ask her to come and listen to what I have been doing. It can be in my home studio, or in the car, or wherever. I watch her face for her initial reaction. Talk about a spontaneous, musical barometer! I can almost always plan on her telling me exactly what she thinks of what I am working on. My advice to anyone planning on a permanent career in music (or perhaps any other area of intense purpose) is to try and find a significant other that is a true friend. Someone that you can trust with everything in life. The best thing that happened to me was to hook up with Bea.

I think Bea is the best person I know, or ever will know, for that matter. I have never had a vision of what we would be together, but I do know that what we mean to each other is vastly more than what either of us could have imagined when we first met. Bea is the light of my life. She is like sunlight, bright and warm, making everything seem clear. She is the most real woman I have ever known. I think that for that very reason, she has made me into a real man!

MILTON T. "BILL" PUTNAM

Bill Putnam on the right at work in the studio in the fifties.

Early in my career, one of my recording industry idols was Milton T., or "Bill," Putnam. He founded Universal Recording Studios in Chicago. Later, Bill moved to California and founded U.R.E.I. — United Recording Electronics Industries (a leading recording electronics manufacturing company). Bill designed some of the greatest, most innovative equipment that we had at the time. But Bill Putnam was also marvelous recording engineer. He was a pioneer. Many of the techniques we use to this day were invented by Bill Putnam. For instance, the way we use reverb or echo in modern recording desks is, in essence, a Bill Putnam brainchild.

Bill Putnam was the father of use of tape repeat, the first vocal booth, the first multiple voice recording, the first 8-track recording trials, experiments with half-speed disc mastering, the design of modern recording desks, the way components are laid out and the way they function, console design, cue sends, echo returns, and multitrack switching.

In 1957, stereo was taking off, and Bill was determined to incorporate many technological innovations into construction on new studios. The United Western studios, still in existence today as both Cello Studios and Allen Sides' Ocean Way Recording, are still considered to be some of the best sounding rooms ever built.

The location and application of the echo send and return controls were first conceived in his fertile imagination. That system has remained almost unchanged from Bill's first, rather small recording consoles to the incredibly powerful mixing desks of today. Many of Bill's accomplishments eventually became standard, common practice in the music recording industry.

Bill Putnam was truly an innovator. He was one of a kind. A bona fide original. I think Bill Putnam had a unique perspective on music recording. He is someone about whom you can rightfully say that he was the first. If you have ever listened to pop music or tried your hand at recording music, Milton T. "Bill" Putnam has touched your life! Bill Putnam is a man who one could easily refer to as the "Father of Music Recording," as we know it today.

In 1956, my wife Bea, my dad and mom, and I were building my studio in Minneapolis. We had bought an old movie theater on Nicollet Avenue. (Which, by the way, is still a state-of-the-art recording studio.) I worked in our studio there for about a year or so. I recorded such notable artists as Bob Davis on an album titled *Jazz from the North Coast* on Geordie Hormel's record label, Zephyr Records. I did some albums with Art Blakey and the Jazz Messengers in that studio that I still hear on the radio. They still sound pretty good, too. I did some interesting sessions there with the Jazz flautist Herbie Mann. I also did some Minnesota-style polka band albums for Decca Records with the famed A&R man Leonard Joy — bands like Whoopee John Wilfhart and Harold Loeffelmacher and the Six Fat Dutchmen. Great fun.

Even with all that excitement, I was beginning to think that I would soon have to leave Minneapolis if I was ever going to be able to do anything truly significant in the music recording industry. In my heart, I knew that what I really wanted to do was to record major musical acts for major record labels.

EDWARD KENNEDY ELLINGTON, AKA "DUKE" ELLINGTON

I recorded the Ellington Band several times during my years at Universal Recording in Chicago. The one group of sessions that stands out in my memory is a few days of work with the Ellington Band starting Thursday, November 29, 1962. As you can see from the following, Duke Ellington made quite an impression on this young 25-year-old Scandinavian kid from Minnesota. I can close my eyes and see him walking into the studio. He had a very regal bearing; the way he carried himself was like he was a member of royalty. When Duke came into the studio, you instantly felt something important was about to happen. And it usually did.

Duke Ellington's music, of course, had preceded him when he entered my life in the recording studio. There are six songs that Duke and his collaborators created that stand out in my musical memory as being some of the most important music in my life: "Mood Indigo," "Sophisticated Lady," "Do Nothin' 'Til You Hear From Me," "Just A-Sittin' and A-Rockin'," "Take The 'A' Train," and "Prelude to a Kiss."

I think you could say that Duke Ellington radiated his being, his personality. He obviously, to me, and everyone else as well, loved his music madly. Music poured from his body and soul. I could tell instantly, the first time that I met Duke Ellington, that he not only loved music, but he lived music! I don't think I have been the same since I met Duke Ellington. Working with him, those few times, made me realize how much music really meant to me. I have worked with many very talented artists in music, but none can compare with Duke Ellington for genuine love of what we do. My personal feeling is that Duke Ellington will go down in history as one of the most important persons in contemporary music. He was both a composer/arranger and a true creator of unique music. In addition to that, he was a very warm, generous human being. A couple of times when I was recording the Ellington Band, I would invite some of my musician pals to come to sit in on the sessions. They would watch the proceedings with their mouths wide open in wonder.

Studio A at Universal Recording in Chicago was a very sizable studio. As I recall, the dimensions were close to 75 feet in length by 50 feet in width, with a 30-foot ceiling height. The control room was raised to the second-story level. To enter the control room you had to go up a flight of stairs. Looking down into the studio from the control room, I remember the "Duke" sitting at the piano during a take with a very thoughtful expression on his face. Then he would scribble a little four-bar riff on a scrap of music paper and quietly tippy-toe around the studio during the take. Of course, he did this while we were actually recording.

He would show this fragment of music paper to the saxes, the trumpets, and then the trombones. At the appropriate musical moment, Duke would stand in the middle of the band, raise his arms and with a great sweeping motion, conduct this little gem, and it would become part of the arrangement. The notes on that little bit of paper would become a part of music history. I always get goosebumps when I think about being a part of events such as this.

The Duke encouraged me to try out my ideas in the studio. If I wanted to try a different mic technique, a new band setup, or whatever, I never got anything but support from him. I watched him closely in the studio. He was perpetually excited about music; he adored his music. When he talked about something new, his eyes lit up and everyone in the room knew that we were on the brink of something fantastic! I wanted to be the same.

QUINCY JONES

I am an only child. I never had a sister or a brother. If I could have anyone that I could think of for a brother, that brother would be Quincy Jones. I don't mean "brother," in the rhetorical manner. I mean brother in the familial way. That doesn't mean that Q and I have always agreed with each other. We have had heated arguments resulting from differences of opinion between us. I don't think that brothers always agree, either. What has made our relationship last is the fact that true friendship, such as ours, is based on mutual respect. I have the ultimate respect for Quincy, on a musical and a personal level.

And I think he feels the same about me. Quincy Jones is the kind of friend that you could call in the middle of the night, with your most personal problem, either real or imagined, and he would come to your rescue, and your life would be on the right track again. I guess what I am trying to say is that I truly love Quincy. In addition, almost everything that I treasure, that I know about recording good music, I have learned from my pal Quincy Jones. Quincy Jones once said about music and how it works on the emotions: "To get out of whatever was distasteful, unpleasant, uncomfortable or painful—music could always soothe that. You just crawl in that world and reach in that black hole and grab something beautiful, and it would take you away from all of that."

Quincy is great fun to be with, in the studio or anywhere. For instance, he loves good food. He loves fine wine. Therefore, Jones and I have a lot in common without going further. Quincy is an authority on the culinary arts. He can also make the most incredible lemon meringue pie you have ever tasted! I think if Q wouldn't have been a giant in the world of music, he would have been one of the world's foremost chefs.

When you are with Q, there is a constant parade of notables passing through the studio. We might be doing an overdub session and I look up and there is Ray Charles sitting in the corner of the control room digging the proceedings, or Jesse Jackson, or Miles Davis, or Dizzy Gillespie, or someone equally famous.

Quincy and I are almost the same age. Actually, Quincy is 13 months older than I am. I have been very careful to point out the fact that I am younger than Q, not only to Quincy, but to anyone else, whenever the opportunity presents itself.

Quincy's approach to his music is kaleidoscopic.

Like Duke Ellington, Quincy's instrument for musical expression is the orchestra. If I were asked to use one unique label for describing Quincy's approach to his music, I would have to use the term "kaleidoscopic." I would say that the terms "fluid" and "buoyant" also come to my mind when I think of the music that we have recorded together. Quincy's way of taking a single piece of music, and making it appear to the ear a certain way on the first listen, and then having a different element in the music to bewitch one's ear on the next listen through, is probably his most unique production technique.

MICHAEL JACKSON

Michael Jackson is the most professional and the most accomplished artist I have ever worked with! And I have worked with the best the music industry has to offer. Michael is a bona fide international favorite, and he has been for a long time! He is unquestionably a survivor. Michael is a gentle soul. He is very polite. Working with him I always hear him use "please," "thank you," and "you're welcome," in an industry where such courtesies are not usually used.

What I can truthfully say is that, first and foremost, Michael is an absolute joy to work with. I can't think of another way to express my experience in working with him. There is no one that I would rather work with. He is the supreme artist. I have never worked with anyone who is more dedicated to his art than Michael. For instance, when we record a vocal on a song, Michael vocalizes with his vocal coach, Seth Riggs, for at least an hour before he steps up to the microphone to record. I don't mean that Michael vocalizes just once in a while. I mean that he vocalizes every time we record a vocal! To me, that is real dedication. One of the most fascinating things about Michael Jackson is the boundless passion that he has for his music. His enthusiasm for the project at hand is like no one else I have ever worked with.

MJ's musical standards are incredibly high. When I work with Michael, we never settle for a musical production that is "just good enough." Since the

Dangerous album project, Michael and I have had a saying that goes, "The quality goes in before the name goes on!" In other words, Michael and I must to be totally satisfied with the musical and technical quality of our productions before we will put our names on them. Of course, Michael is not the kid next door!

Looking back at my early years growing up in Minnesota makes me realize that it was quite common among my friends and relatives not to get excited about occupation or profession. To this day I don't know why. No one ever spoke to me of keeping my interest in my work conservative. I learned that it was OK to like what you did for a living, but to really get excited about your life's work just wasn't done.

To illustrate this kind of thinking, here's a little story that stands out clearly in my memory. I think this happened about 1954 or 1955 (I was about18 years old). I distinctly remember asking one of my cousins in Minneapolis about how his work was going. His reply to me was, "Well it's going OK, I guess, I'm doing my best not to get involved." I thought to myself, "You poor, sad-ass working stiff! I'm going to make sure that I never think like that."

DISCOGRAPHY

GJALLARHORN, *Rimfaxe*
Album released March 1, 2006
Vindauga Music

SONGS:
"Rimfaxe"
"Kokkovirsi"
"Systrana"
"Blacken"
"Hymn"
"Sylvklar"
"Norafjelds"
"I Vall"
"Taklax 1037"
"Taklax 1034"
"Staffan"
"Graning"

JENNIFER LOPEZ, *Rebirth*
Album released March 1, 2005
Epic Records

SONGS:
"Get Right"
"Step into My World"
"Hold You Down (Featuring Fat Joe)"
"Whatever You Wanna Do"
"Cherry Pie"
"I Got U"
"Still Around"
"Ryde or Die"
"I, Love"
"He'll Be Back"
"(I Can't Believe) This Is Me"
"Get Right (Featuring Fabulous)"

JENNIFER LOPEZ, *This Is Me ... Then*
Album released November 26, 2002
Epic Records

SONGS:
"Still"
"Glad"
"Ben"
"I'm Good"
"All I Have" (Featuring L. L. Cool J)
"I've Been Thinking"
"You Belong To Me"
"The One"
"Baby I Love You"
"All My Life"
"Jenny from the Block"

Single #1 (Sept 2002): "Jenny from the Block"
Single #2 (Jan 2003): "All I Have" (Featuring L. L. Cool J)
#1 on Billboard Magazine's Hot 100 music chart for five consecutive weeks

SANTANA, *Shaman*
Album released October, 2002
Epic Records

SONGS:
"Nothing At All" (Featuring Musiq)

MICHAEL JACKSON, *1978 to 2001: The Epic Releases*
Off the Wall
Thriller
Bad
Dangerous
HIStory
Invincible

NOTE: All the Michael Jackson singles are at least Top 5 pop hits. Most peaked at number one.

Off the Wall
Album released August 10, 1979

SONGS:
"Don't Stop 'Til You Get Enough"—6:04
"Rock with You"—3:40
"Working Day and Night"—5:04
"Get on the Floor"—4:57
"Off the Wall"—4:06
"Girlfriend"—3:04
"She's Out of My Life"—3:38
"I Can't Help It"—4:29
"It's the Falling in Love"—3:48
"Burn this Disco Out"—3:48

Single (Sep. 1979): "Don't Stop 'Til You Get Enough"
Single (Nov. 1979): "Off the Wall"
Single (Nov. 1979): "Rock with You"
Single (Apr. 1980): "She's out of My Life"

Thriller
Album released November 30, 1982
NOTE: *Thriller* is the biggest-selling album in the history of recorded music.

SONGS:
"Wanna Be Startin' Something"—6:02
"Baby Be Mine"—4:20
"The Girl Is Mine"—3:42
"Thriller"—5:57
"Beat It"—4:17
"Billie Jean"—4:57
"Human Nature"—4:05
"P.Y.T. (Pretty Young Thing)"—3:58
"The Lady in My Life"—4:57

Single (Dec. 1982): "The Girl Is Mine"
Single (Feb. 1983): "Billie Jean"
Single (April 1983): "Beat It"
Single (Jun. 1983): "Wanna Be Startin' Something"

Single (Aug. 1983): "Human Nature"
Single (Oct. 1983): "Pretty Young Thing (P.Y.T.)"
Single (Dec. 1983): "Thriller"

Bad

Album released August 28, 1987
NOTE: *Bad* is the first album in the history of recorded music to have five consecutive number-one pop hits by a single artist.

Songs:
"Bad" — 4:06
"The Way You Make Me Feel" — 4:58
"Speed Demon" — 4:01
"Liberian Girl"- 3:52
"Just Good Friends" — 4:05
"Another Part of Me" — 3:53
"Man in the Mirror" — 5:18
"I Just Can't Stop Loving You" — 4:23
"Dirty Diana " — 4:52
"Smooth Criminal" — 4:16

Single (July 1987) — "I Just Can't Stop Loving You"
Single (Sept 1987) — "Bad"
Single (Nov 1987) — "The Way You Make Me Feel"
Single (Jan 1988) — "Man in the Mirror"
Single (March 1988) — "Dirty Diana"
Single (May 1988) — "Another Part of Me"
Single (Jan 1989) — "Smooth Criminal"
Single (March 1989) — "Leave Me Alone"

Dangerous

Album released November 22, 1991
NOTE: Co-composer of one song, "Jam"; co-produced five songs and recorded and mixed 11 songs.

Songs:
"Jam"- 5:39
"Why You Wanna Trip on Me"- 5:29
"In the Closet"- 6:32
"She Drives Me Wild"- 3:42

"Remember the Time" — 4:01
"Can't Let Her Get Away" — 5:02
"Heal the World" — 6:24
"Black or White" — 4:16
"Who Is It?" — 6:36
"Give in to Me" — 5:29
"Will You Be There" — 7:40
"Keep the Faith" — 5:57
"Gone Too Soon" — 3:23
"Dangerous" — 7:00

Single (Nov. 1991): "Remember the Time"
Single (Jan. 1992): "In the Closet"
Single (May 1992): "Who Is It?"
Single (Aug. 1992): "Jam"
Single (Oct. 1992): "Heal the World"
Single (Jan. 1993): "Give in to Me"
Single (April 1993): "Will You Be There"
Single (July 1993): "Gone Too Soon"

HIStory: Past, Present, and Future
Two-CD album released June, 1995
NOTE: Co-composer of two songs:"2 BAD" and "This Time Around"; co-produced three songs and recorded and mixed 28 songs.

SONGS:
DISC A:
"Billie Jean" — 4:57
"The Way You Make Me Feel" — 4:58
"Black or White"- 4:15
"Rock with You" — 3:40
"She's Out of My Life" — 3:38
"Bad" — 4:05
"I Just Can't Stop Loving You" — 4:05
"Man in the Mirror" — 4:55
"Thriller" — 5:57
"Beat It" — 4:17
"The Girl Is Mine" — 3:42
"Remember the Time" — 3:59
"Don't Stop 'Til You Get Enough" — 6:04

"Wanna Be Startin' Something" — 6:02
"Heal the World" — 6:25
Disc B:
"Scream" — 4:37
"They Don't Care About Us" — 4:44
"Stranger in Moscow" — 5:43
"This Time Around" — 4:20
"Earth Song" — 6:45
"D.S." — 4:49
"Money" — 4:49
"Come Together" — 5:27
"You Are Not Alone" — 5:45
"Childhood" — 4:27
"Tabloid Junkie" — 4:32
"2 Bad" — 4:49
"HIStory" — 6:37
"Little Susie" — 6:13
"Smile" — 4:55

Single (June 1995): "Scream"
Single (Aug. 1995): "You Are Not Alone"
Single (Nov. 1995): "Earth Song"
Single (Mar. 1996): "They Don't Care About Us"
Single (Sep. 1996): "Stranger in Moscow"

Invincible
Album released October 30, 2001, 1995

Songs:
"Unbreakable" — 6:26
"Heartbreaker" — 5:09
"Invincible" — 4:46
"Break of Dawn" — 5:36
"Heaven Can Wait" — 4:46
"You Rock My World" — 5:39
"Butterflies" — 4:42
"Speechless" — 3:20
"2000 Watts" — 4:25
"Shout!" — 4:17
"Don't Walk Away" — 4:24

"Privacy" — 5:04
"Cry" (R. Kelly) — 5:02
"The Lost Children" — 3:45
"Whatever Happens" — 4:55
"Threatened" — 4:15

Single (Sep. 2001): "You Rock My World"

Plus
"The Making of Michael Jackson's *Thriller*"

Moonwalker
Full-length feature film

SYLK-E FYNE, *Ya Style*
Album, 2001
RuffTown Entertainment

CYRIUS, *Le Sang des Roses*
Album, 2000
Sony Music/Columbia Records, France
(Recorded at Egrem Studios in Havana, Cuba)

LES GO, *Dan Gna*
Album, 2000
Juna Records
(Les Go are a young, internationally-acclaimed female dance and vocal trio
from the Ivory Coast who sing in Manding, French, and English.)

ANA TORROJA, *Pasajes De Un Sueno*
Album, 1999
BMG Records, Spain

NILS LANDGREN, *5000 Miles*
Album, 1999
ACT Records

HERBIE HANCOCK, *Gershwin's World*
Album, 1998
Verve Records

ANTONIO CHAINHO, *A Guitarra*
Album, 1998
MoviepLay Records, Portugal

CARLINHOS BROWN
Album, 1998
EMI Records, Brazil

NICOLE RENEE, *Nicole Renee*
Album, 1998
Atlantic Records

SINGLE:
"Strawberry"

QUINCY JONES — *1958 to the Present*
Qwest/Warner Bros. Records

ALBUMS:
Back on the Block
Q's Jook Joint
SINGLE:
"You Put a Move on My Heart"

A&M RECORDS

ALBUMS:
Sounds and Stuff Like That
Roots
The Dude
SINGLES:
"I Heard That!"
"Stuff Like That"
"Ai No Corrida"
"Just Once"
"Betcha' Wouldn't Hurt Me"

MERCURY RECORDS: Several major artists, including Dinah Washington.
Quincy Jones, Music for the Television Series *Roots*, 1976
    Produced by Quincy Jones
    Wolper Productions

DAVID HASSELHOFF, *You Are Everything*
    Album, 1993
    BMG-Ariola Records, Germany

    SONGS (composed, co-produced, recorded, and mixed):
    "The Best Is Yet to Come"
    "Miracle of Love"
    "San Pedros' Children"
    "Hit and Run"
    Songs (co-produced, recorded, and mixed):
    "You Are Everything"
    "'Til the Last Teardrop Falls"

DOUG STONE, *More Love*
    Album, 1992
    Epic Records

    SONG (co-produced and mixed):
    "Dream High"

SKO/TORP, *Familiar Roads*
    Album, co-produced and mixed
    EMI-Medley Records, Denmark

    SINGLE:
    "Familiar Roads"

BARBRA STREISAND
    Columbia Records

    SINGLES:
    "The Places You Find Love"
    "'Til I Loved You"

SERGIO MENDES, *Brasileiro*
Elektra Records

SINGLE:
"What Is This?" (Also arranged by Bruce Swedien)

SERGIO MENDES, *Sergio Mendes*
A&M Records
"Confetti"

SINGLES:
"Never Gonna Let You Go"
"Olympia"
"Alibis"

KYUSOKE HIMURU, *Master Piece*
Five songs on album
Co-produced with Hero Suzuki
EMI Japan

JENNIFER HOLLIDAY, *Say You Love Me*
Geffen Records

SINGLE:
"You're the One" (Produced by Michael Jackson)

HERB ALPERT, *Blow Your Own Horn*
Album, 1983
A&M Records

SINGLE:
"Garden Party"

RENÉ AND ANGELA, *Street Called Desire*
(Engineered and co-produced)
Polygram Records

SINGLES:
"Save Your Love for Number One"
"I'll Be Good"
"Your Smile"
"You Don't Have to Cry"

MISSING PERSONS, *Rhyme and Reason*
Album produced by Missing Persons and Bruce Swedien
Capitol Records

SINGLE:
"Give"
Videos:"Give"
"Right Now"

THE JACKSONS, *Victory*
Epic Records

SINGLE:
"State of Shock"

JAMES INGRAM, *It's Your Night*
Qwest Records

SINGLES:
"Party Animal"
"There's No Easy Way"
"Yah Mo B There"
"Find 100 Ways"

DONNA SUMMER, *Donna Summer*
Geffen Records

SINGLES:
"Love is in Control (Finger on the Trigger)"
"The Woman in Me"
"State of Independence"

GEORGE BENSON, *Give Me the Night*
Qwest/Warner Records

SINGLES:
"Give Me the Night"
"Love Times Love"

PATTI AUSTIN, *Every Home Should Have One*
Qwest Records

SINGLES:
"Baby, Come to Me" (duet with James Ingram)
"Every Home Should Have One"

LENA HORNE, *The Lady and Her Music (Live on Broadway)*
Qwest Records

VIDEO:
"The Lady and Her Music" (two-hour TV special)
SINGLE:
"Stormy Weather"

RUFUS AND CHAKA KAHN, *Masterjam*
MCA Records

SINGLES:
"Do You Love What You Feel?"
"Any Love"

ROBERTA FLACK, *"Making Love"*
Single (Produced by Burt Bacharach)
Atlantic Records

ERNIE WATTS, *Chariots of Fire*
Qwest Records

WOODY HERMAN, 1959 to 1962
STAN KENTON, 1959 to 1965
Capitol Records

COUNT BASIE, 1960 to 1965
Several albums, including *Nothin' But the Blues* (Count Basie Band with Joe Williams), *Basie On The Beatles*, and many more.

OSCAR PETERSON, 1959 TO 1965
Roulette Records
Many albums, including the *Composer Series*
Verve Records—Norman Granz

DUKE ELLINGTON, 1959 to 1965
Several albums, including individual songs with Billy Strayhorn.

SARAH VAUGHN, 1963 to 1992
Solo album with Lalo Schifrin on Roulette Records
Album with Quincy Jones: *Back on the Block*

EDDIE HARRIS, 1959 to 1976
Vee-Jay Records
Exodus

ATLANTIC RECORDS
Bad Luck Is All I Have
Listen Here
That Is Why You're Overweight
Love Is Too Much to Touch
Plus many more

JOHNNY JANIS, 1965
Solo album with Don Costa on Monument Records

KEN NORDINE, 1959 to 1976

ALBUMS:
Word Jazz
Twink
Colors
CBS Radio Show: "Now, Nordine"
Plus many more

YOUNG-HOLT TRIO, 1960
Chess Records
"The Inn Crowd"
"Soulful Strut"
Plus many more

JULIE LONDON, 1960

SINGLE:
"Desafinado"

LOUIE PRIMA AND KEELY SMITH, 1959
Capitol Records

ALBUM:
Swingin' Pretty
SINGLES:
"I've Got You Under My Skin"

FRANKIE VALLI AND THE FOUR SEASONS, 1961

SINGLES:
"Big Girls Don't Cry"
Plus many more

JERRY BUTLER, 1962
Vee-Jay Records
"Moon River"
Plus many more

BETTY EVERETT, 1963
"The Shoop Shoop Song"

JACKIE WILSON, 1963
Brunswick Records
"Higher and Higher"
Plus many more

RAMSEY LEWIS, 1963
Chess Records

ALBUM:
Wade in the Water
SINGLE:
"The Inn Crowd"

GENE CHANDLER, 1963
"Duke of Earl"
Plus many more

PHIL FORD AND MIMI HINES, 1965
MGM Records
Produced by Don Costa

BARBARA ACKLIN, 1965
Brunswick Records
"Love Makes a Woman"
Plus many more

BUDDY MILES, 1970
Mercury Records
"Them Changes"
"Down by the River"
Plus many more

TYRONE DAVIS, 1968 to 1977
Six albums
Dakar Records

SINGLES:
"Turn Back the Hands of Time"
"Can I Change My Mind?"
"There It Is"
Plus many more

THE CHI-LITES, 1970 to 1975
Six albums
Brunswick Records

SINGLES:
"Have You Seen Her?"
"Oh Girl"
"More Power to the People"
"Coldest Days of My Life"
Plus many more

LIONEL HAMPTON, 1972
Brunswick Records

NATALIE COLE, *Inseparable*
Album, 1974

SINGLE:
"Inseparable"

LESLIE GORE, *Love Me By Name*
Album, 1976
A&M Records
(Produced by Quincy Jones)

SINGLE:
"Love Me By Name"

THE BROTHERS JOHNSON, 1976 to 1983
A&M Records
(Produced by Quincy Jones)

ALBUMS:
Look Out for Number One
Blam
Light Up the Night
SINGLES:
"I'll Be Good to You"
"Get the Funk Out Ma Face"
"Ain't We Funkin' Now?"
"Stomp"

BILLY ECKSTINE, 1976
A&M Records
(Produced by Quincy Jones)
"Getaway (Faraway Forever)"
"The Best Thing"

MOTION PICTURE SCORES AND SOUNDTRACK ALBUMS

The Wiz, 1978
  Motion picture score and soundtrack album
  Music produced by Quincy Jones
  Motion picture score for Universal Pictures
  Soundtrack album for MCA Records
  Singles:"Ease on Down the Road"
  "Home"

Running Scared
  Motion picture score and soundtrack album
  Music produced by Rod Temperton, Dick Rudolph, and Bruce Swedien
  MGM Pictures
  Soundtrack album for MCA Records
  Album and soundtrack co-produced and engineered

  SINGLES:
  "Sweet Freedom" — Michael McDonald
  "Man-Sized Love" — Klymaxx

The Color Purple
  Motion picture score and soundtrack album
  (Executive-produced and engineered the soundtrack album)
  Warner Bros. and Qwest Records

Night Shift
  Motion picture score and soundtrack album
  Music composed and produced by Burt Bacharach
  A Ladd Company Release

PARTIAL LIST OF ARTISTS RECORDED AND MIXED

Barbara Acklin	Patti Austin
Bobby Blue Bland	Oscar Brown Jr.
Jerry Butler	David Carroll
Gene Chandler	Chi-Lites
Herman Clebanoff	Nat "King" Cole
Natalie Cole	Don Costa
King Curtis	Tyrone Davis
Donny Hathaway	Jimmy Dorsey
Tommy Dorsey	Betty Everett

Roberta Flack
Eydie Gormé
Tito Guizar
John Lee Hooker
James Ingram
Johnny Janis
Mick Jagger
Jennifer Holliday
Quincy Jones
Anita Kerr
Julie London
LTD
Paul McCartney
Sergio Mendes
Bob Newhart
Andre Previn
Jimmy Reed
Rufus and Chaka Khan
Soupy Sales
Lalo Schifrin
The Smothers Brothers
Donna Summer
Sarah Vaughn
Muddy Waters
Jackie Wilson
Si Zentner

Phil Ford and Mimi Hines
Leslie Gore
The Hi-Los
Lena Horne
Michael Jackson
The Jacksons
Gordon Jenkins
The Brothers Johnson
Lainie Kazan
Peggy King
Jennifer Lopez
Norman Luboff
Curtis Mayfield
Buddy Miles
Ohio Players
Louie Prima and Keely Smith
Diana Ross
Nipsey Russell
Tommy Sands
Dinah Shore
Barbra Streisand
Dana Valery
Dinah Washington
Johnny "Guitar" Watson
Edgar Winter
Frankie Valli and the Four Seasons

CLASSICAL ARTISTS
Rolf Bjoerling
The Fine Arts Quartet
The Chicago Symphony Orchestra
The Chicago Strings
The Chicago Symphony String Quartet
The Pro Musica Quartet
Saint Olaf Choir

DIXIELAND JAZZ ARTISTS
Dukes of Dixieland
Bill Reinhardt and Jazz Limited

Dave Remington
Bob Scobey
Jack Teagarden

JAZZ ARTISTS

Count Basie	Art Blakey
Duke Ellington	Dizzy Gillespie
Lionel Hampton	Eddie Harris
Woody Herman	Earl "Fatha" Hines
Quincy Jones	Stan Kenton
Ramsey Lewis	Herbie Mann
Oscar Peterson	Ernie Watts
Joe Williams	Herbie Hancock

ASSORTED CREDITS: ENGINEER, PRODUCER,
ASSOCIATE PRODUCER, AND RECORDING AND MIXING

1982: *Night Shift* Original Soundtrack
   Recording and mixing

1984: *Rhyme & Reason*, Missing Persons

1985: *Color Purple* Original Soundtrack
   Engineer, executive producer

1985: *Street Called Desire*, René & Angela
   Producer, recording, and mixing

1986: *Running Scared* Original Soundtrack
   Producer, recordng and mixing

1986: *Sweet Freedom: The Best of Michael McDonald*, Michael McDonald
   Producer, recording, and mixing

1987: *Best of Missing Persons*, Missing Persons
   Producer, recording and mixing

1987: Sergio Mendes and Brasil '66
   Associate producer, recording

1992: *Brasileiro*, Sergio Mendes
   Arranger, recording and mixing

1992: *Dangerous*, Michael Jackson
   Arranger, vocals, producer, recording and mixing

1993: *Hell Collection*, Sparks
  Producer, recording and mixing

1993: *More Love*, Doug Stone
  Producer, recording and mixing

1995: *Free Willy* Original Soundtrack
  Producer, engineer, executive producer, recording and mixing

1995: *Gordy* Original Soundtrack
  Producer, recording and mixing

1995: *Looking for the Best*, David Hasselhoff
  Composer, producer, recording and mixing

1997: *Street Called Desire and More*, René & Angela
  Producer, engineer, recording and mixing

1998: *A Guitarra*, Antonio Chainho
  Recording and mixing

1999: *From Q with Love*, Quincy Jones
  Drums, engineer, recording and mixing

2001: *Bad,* Michael Jackson (Bonus tracks)
  Drums, engineer, executive producer, recording and mixing, and announcer

2001:*Very Best of Michael McDonald*, Michael McDonald
  Recording and mixing, and original recording producer

2001: *Dangerous* (Remastered), Michael Jackson
  Synthesizer, arranger, recording and mixing, producer

2001: *Off the Wall* (Bonus Tracks), Michael Jackson
  Executive producer, recording and mixing, compilation

2004: *Butterfly in a Blizzard*, Amanda
  Producer, recording and mixing

2004: *Ultimate Collection*, Michael Jackson
  Arranger, producer, effects, recording and mixing

Plus many, many more.

HONORS AND AWARDS

Bruce Swedien has been nominated for a total of thirteen Grammys, and has won five. He has also been awarded ten Grammy certificates and two ASCAP composer awards, and has been nominated for four TEC (Technical Excellence and Creativity) awards by the Mix Foundation. In 1991, he was honored with the TEC Hall Of Fame Lifetime Achievement award.

On November 10, 2001, Bruce Swedien was awarded the Honorary Doctor of Philosophy degree from Luleå University of Technology in Luleå, Sweden, presented under ruling of King Carl XVI Gustav. Swedien, a Minnesota-born descendent of Swedish immigrants, is the first in the music industry to receive this auspicious honor.

TEC AWARDS
1991 "Hall Of Fame": Lifetime Achievement Award
1983 — 1991 "TEC awards": Nominated four times

GRAMMY NOMINATIONS AND AWARDS
1962: "Big Girls Don't Cry" (Single)
Frankie Valli and the Four Seasons

1969: *Moog Groove* (Album)
Electronic Concept Orchestra

Best Engineered Recording category
1978: *Sounds and Stuff Like That* (Album)
Quincy Jones

Best Engineered Recording category
1980: *Give Me the Night* (Album)
George Benson

Best Engineered Recording category
1981: *The Dude* (Album)
Quincy Jones

Best Engineered Recording category
1983: *Thriller* (Album) — Won!
Michael Jackson

Best Engineered Recording category
1987: *Bad* (Album) — Won!
Michael Jackson

Best Engineered Recording category
1990: *Back on the Block* (Album) — Won!
Quincy Jones

Best Engineered Recording category
1992: *Dangerous* (Album) — Won!
Michael Jackson

Best Engineered Recording category
1992: "Jam" — (Composer, with Rene Moore,
    Michael Jackson, and Teddy Riley)

Best Rhythm and Blues Song, Songwriters Award
1995: *HIStory: Past, Present, and Future, Book I* (Album)
Michael Jackson

Producer category
1995: *HIStory: Past, Present, and Future, Book I* (Album)
Michael Jackson

Best Engineered Recording category
1996: *Q's Jook Joint* (Album) — Won!
Quincy Jones

Best Engineered Recording category

ASCAP AWARDS
1992: "Jam"
Bruce Swedien, Top Ten Writer
Artist: Michael Jackson

1992: "Jam"
Bruce Swedien, Top Ten Publisher
Artist: Michael Jackson

Altogether I have
won five Grammys.

INDEX

For the most part, this is an index of people mentioned in this book. There are also some references to trademarks of certain importance to the whole story.

ABOUT THE AUTHOR

Five-time Grammy winner Bruce Swedien's career in music recording began with the music of the post-swing era and continues through today's multimedia digital technology. First publicly recognized in 1962 with a Grammy nomination for Frankie Valli and the Four Seasons' "Big Girls Don't Cry," Bruce went on to record and mix Michael Jackson's *Thriller*, the best-selling album in the history of recorded music. (104 million copies so far, according to Guinness.)

Bruce was born in Minneapolis, Minnesota. He graduated high school from Minnehaha Academy in Minneapolis, and studied electrical engineering with a minor in music at the University of Minnesota. He studied classical piano technique with private teachers from age 10 to age 18. Bruce married Beatrice Anderson soon after graduation from high school.

He began his recording interest with the gift of a disc recording machine from his father on his tenth birthday. Ten minutes later, he decided on music recording as a career. At the age of 14, Bruce began working in a small basement recording studio in Minneapolis on evenings, weekends, and summer vacations. He continued this activity all through his high school years. Upon graduation from high school, he bought his first professional tape recorder (a Magnacord Model PT-6), which he used continually to learn more about music recording.

During his university and early marriage years, he worked in and around Minneapolis, recording jazz groups, choirs, polka bands, commercials for radio, and assorted music groups. During the summer of 1953, Bruce tried briefly to work as a disc jockey for a small radio station in nearby Wisconsin, but he always seemed to end up somewhere with his tape recorder, recording some willing musical group. Bruce came back to Minneapolis to continue his formal education, and while doing so, took a full-time job as operator of the Schmitt Music Company's recording facility. There, he had the opportunity of working for the first time with major recording artists such as Tito Guizar and Tommy Dorsey.

Operating a recording studio worked so well that he bought the equipment and business from Schmitt's and moved the facility to a large, old movie theater on Nicollet Avenue in Minneapolis. He was then 19 years old and bursting with ambition and energy. It took a lot of both to mold the old movie theater into the fine recording studio that it soon became (it still is a world-class recording studio).

In 1957, Bruce moved with wife Bea and their three children to Chicago, to work for RCA Victor recording studios. While there, he did several recordings with the Chicago Symphony Orchestra. During this period, he recorded Jimmy Dorsey's last recording, released on the Dot Label. Bruce worked for RCA for 11 months. During that time, Bill Putnam's Universal Recording at Chicago was completing its new, large facilities at 46 East Walton.

From 1958 to 1967, Bruce worked on staff for Universal Recording Studios in Chicago. During that period, he recorded every major artist that recorded in the Windy City, among them Count Basie, Stan Kenton, Duke Ellington, Woody Herman, Oscar Peterson, Sarah Vaughan, Dinah Washington, and many more. During that time, he met and worked with Quincy Jones, a relationship that has happily lasted to the present time.

Since going independent in 1969, Bruce has been doing the major share of his projects in New York and Los Angeles on record albums and motion pictures scores. He moved his residence and business to the Los Angeles area in December of 1975. In June of 1977, he went to New York to work with Quincy Jones on the motion picture *The Wiz*. It was on this occasion that he met and began working with Michael Jackson.

Bruce has done projects with New York– and Los Angeles–based producers and artists such as Michael Jackson, Quincy Jones, Burt Bacharach, Herb Alpert, Sergio Mendes, Rene Moore, and many more. He has produced and co-produced the music for several albums and motion picture scores. Bruce moved his residence and business to the New York area in May of 1994.

During the past few years, he has authored many articles for major recording industry journals and magazines. He has conducted a master class in music engineering for the University of California, Los Angeles, and recently did a very successful residency for California State University in Fresno, California. In April of 2002, Bruce moved his residence and business to the Ocala, Florida area.

He has done many lectures and music recording seminars for universities, colleges, and other organizations, including the Audio Engineering Society and the National Academy of Recording Arts and Sciences here in America, and industry societies in Sweden, Denmark, Norway, Finland, Japan, Germany, Canada, and Mexico City, Mexico.

In the autumn of 2003, Bruce published his book *Make Mine Music*. In it, Bruce tells his story in his own words. If you've ever wanted to be a fly on the wall at a Duke Ellington session, or wondered what a typical session with Michael Jackson is like, Bruce's book will tell you. What's more, Swedien generously gives away detailed information from his lifetime in the studio, including insights into psychoacoustics, how he approaches the stereo soundfield, microphone selection and placement techniques, the art of mixing, and the role of technology in capturing musical inspiration. An invaluable research tool for the recording musician, engineer and producer, *Make Mine Music* is also an incredibly engaging and entertaining read, no matter what your level of technical expertise and interest.